Men, Money
and
Chocolate

Men, Money
and
Chocolate

A tale about pursuing love, success and pleasure,
and how to be happy before you have it all...

MENNA VAN PRAAG

HAY HOUSE

Australia • Canada • Hong Kong • India
South Africa • United Kingdom • United States

Published and distributed in the United Kingdom by:

Hay House UK Ltd, 292B Kensal Rd, London W10 5BE. Tel.: (44) 20 8962 1230; Fax: (44)
20 8962 1239. www.hayhouse.co.uk

Published and distributed in the United States of America by:

Hay House, Inc., PO Box 5100, Carlsbad, CA 92018-5100. Tel.: (1) 760 431 7695 or
(800) 654 5126; Fax: (1) 760 431 6948 or (800) 650 5115. www.hayhouse.com

Published and distributed in Australia by:

Hay House Australia Ltd, 18/36 Ralph St, Alexandria NSW 2015. Tel.: (61) 2 9669 4299;
Fax: (61) 2 9669 4144. www.hayhouse.com.au

Published and distributed in the Republic of South Africa by:

Hay House SA (Pty), Ltd, PO Box 990, Witkoppen 2068. Tel./Fax: (27) 11 467 8904.
www.hayhouse.co.za

Published and distributed in India by:

Hay House Publishers India, Muskaan Complex, Plot No.3, B-2, Vasant Kunj, New Delhi
– 110 070. Tel.: (91) 11 4176 1620; Fax: (91) 11 4176 1630. www.hayhouse.co.in

Distributed in Canada by:

Raincoast, 9050 Shaughnessy St, Vancouver, BC V6P 6E5. Tel.: (1) 604 323 7100; Fax:
(1) 604 323 2600

First self-published in 2008
© Menna van Praag, 2009

A catalogue record for this book is available from the British Library.

ISBN 978-1-84850-084-6

Printed in the UK by CPI Bookmarque, Croydon, CR0 4TD.

For Artur, my love, my light

Go to that place of silence within.
You'll feel the vastness of the world
And its limitless possibilities.
You'll know you can do anything,
And have everything.
You will see that right now
You are perfect, exactly as you are.

A Note on Self-Judgment

When this story begins, the protagonist, Maya, hates her life but doesn't know how to change it. Trapped in fear, doubt and negative thoughts, she doesn't believe she will ever have a life she loves.

Then she meets a series of extraordinary people who show her some of the secrets to happiness. With their help Maya finds the courage and passion to create her own joyful life.

But in the beginning Maya is still stuck in self-pity. This might feel uncomfortable to read, especially if you're sometimes hard on yourself and hold yourself to very high standards. You may notice feeling annoyed with her, judging her for being stuck, just as you may judge yourself for similar 'faults'.

However, when you join Maya on her journey, you'll start to discover how to be kind to yourself. And, as you accept and love her, to have compassion for her suffering, you can learn to love yourself unconditionally too.

And, of course, unconditional love is one of the deepest, most essential secrets to happiness of all...

cs Maya stepped into The Cocoa Café her heart sank a little. Every morning was the same. She woke while it was still dark, dressed and drank coffee, before walking slowly down the stairs connecting her flat to the café. Then she spent the next few hours baking, until the first customer rang the bell.

The café had been her mother's dream, and as a little girl Maya had loved it. She'd helped to bake, sweep and serve. She sat behind the counter while her mother, Lily, was busy, staring at the door and leaping up whenever it opened.

Maya had loved cutting thick slices of chocolate-cherry tarts, raspberry pavlovas and lemon drizzle cakes. She had offered customers fresh lavender-sugar doughnuts and iced citrus biscuits. She'd smiled to see people's eyes light up as she slid their treats across the old oak counter.

When Maya turned eighteen she finally felt ready to leave the warmth of the café and go out into the world. She'd won a place at Oxford to read English Literature and couldn't wait to go. It was all she could talk about. Customers congratulated her, and Maya gave them free chocolate cupcakes in return. Lily was so proud of her daughter she named the 'treat of the week' Trinity Tiramisu in Maya's honour and kept it on the special's board all summer.

Oxford was everything Maya had dreamt it would be. She walked among words, spent her days sitting in stories, and her nights creating new tales for the characters in her dreams.

She read every piece of literature she could find, working her way alphabetically along the library shelves, hiding herself away in the maze of corridors that contained at least one copy of every book ever printed.

One night, when Maya was studying late in the library, she stumbled upon a very special book.

Hours later, when she finally put it down, Maya gazed out of the window and smiled at the stars. She knew then that she had finally found her place in the world. She knew then that she was a writer. In the silence Maya had heard her soul speak, and she'd felt truly alive for the first time: as bright as lightning and as light as air.

After that she wrote all the time. She filled notebooks so quickly that soon hundreds were scattered across her bedroom floor. Any piece of paper became a page. Maya scribbled novels on napkins, receipts and ticket stubs, sometimes surprising herself with sentences so beautiful and true they took her breath away.

However, six months after Maya left home Lily fell ill. At first they didn't know what it was. At first there was still hope. But two months after that, when the diagnosis had been confirmed, Maya dropped out of Oxford to come home and take care of her. Lily had lived until Christmas Eve, and the night she died asked Maya to take care of the café.

That was ten years ago, and Maya tried not to think about it now: the day she lost her mother and the moment she lost herself. But the pain still lingered in her heart, nestled in a dark, wet corner that throbbed whenever she remembered.

Maya sighed as she crossed the floor, passing empty shelves that would soon be sinking under the weight of cakes and chocolate flapjacks, and dropped step by step down the stairs to the café kitchen. There she stayed, bent over bowls, lining cake tins, opening ovens, snacking on honey and chocolate chips, until the sun came up.

After opening, Maya made herself a cappuccino and sat behind the café counter to stare out at the rain. She watched people rushing past, hiding under their umbrellas and pushing through the wind.

Every day Maya lost an ongoing battle to resist breakfasting on coffee and chocolate croissants. Sometimes she managed to hold back for a few hours, but rarely made it to ten o'clock without devouring a couple of croissants in a guilt-laden frenzy. The rest of the day was an inevitable downslide into oblivion. All the time the chocolate treats tempted her, and Maya wondered desperately why she couldn't win a battle of wills with a slice of fudge cake, just once.

She glanced at a plate of chocolate cupcakes on the counter and absolutely vowed that today she wouldn't eat anything sweet. She looked down at the unopened self-help book in her hands, the title promising to cure Maya of her addiction to unavailable men, and caught the sad sight of her cake-rounded belly under her apron. Maya turned a page, trying to focus, but her heart wasn't in it.

Some days Maya feared she'd finally have to let go of her dreams. For years she'd been trying to finish a novel, scribbling sentences between baking cakes, serving customers and worrying about her accounts. She'd tried, hoped and wished to find love but had spent the last decade either serially single or recovering from failed love affairs. And every day she tried to impose a strict diet on herself, calling on ever-diminishing reserves of willpower, and every day she succumbed to temptation.

Maya's world was shaped by her thoughts about men, money and chocolate; and these thoughts were almost always self-critical and depressing. In the pursuit of love, success and weight loss she'd failed to find anything like joy, but she continued to try. It rarely occurred to Maya that perhaps she might be mistaken, that in her obsessive focus on these particular goals she may be missing something.

Sometimes Maya sensed some special secret to happiness that lay just beyond her reach. For, in rare moments, she would be surprised by a sensation of childhood joy that crept up when her head hovered over a cake bowl and she bent down to sniff the sugar, or caught the sight of sunlight through golden leaves. Without knowing why or how, the memory of something she'd once known would touch her and suddenly she would smile, seeing a whole bright and brilliant world opening up before her. And for one eternal moment Maya would be flooded with a feeling of warmth and peace. But in the next second it was gone.

So, while Maya believed, deep in her heart, that she could be truly happy, she had absolutely no idea how.

Maya sipped her cappuccino and glanced around the café. In her mother's day it had been full of people, noisy with happy chatter. But nowadays it was often empty.

Maya worried that she wasn't paying off her debts fast enough. In the first few years after Lily died Maya had made some heavy mistakes. Ten years on they weighed on her still, not helped by the number of chain coffee shops that multiplied through the town like a genetic cloning project set on world domination. Every week at least three new ones seemed to spring up in a single street.

But, for now at least, Maya was holding on, slowly pulling herself from the brink of financial collapse. Her regulars were loyal. They'd been loyal to her mother and they were loyal to her. At least they would be as long as she kept making Lily's famous flapjacks and adding chocolate-covered cocoa beans to their cappuccinos.

Maya stared at a lone couple sitting in the corner, snuggling into soft, red velvet cushions. The man whispered into the girl's ear and she giggled. Maya looked away and reached for a cupcake. The sight of two people in love, when she had no one, was too much to bear without the comfort of chocolate.

Maya's thoughts turned, as they usually did in moments like these, to Jake.

Jake was a customer Maya fantasised about on a regular basis. She spent hours imagining the same glorious scenario, the two of them together in an exquisitely expensive flat in Paris, bathing in champagne and feeding each other strawberries. To this daydream she added an ability to indulge in vast quantities of chocolate cake, while being completely unable to put on a single pound. Sometimes Maya varied things a little, usually the locations.

Jake was tall, blond and heart-stoppingly gorgeous. Indeed, Maya often thought he was a little too gorgeous for his own good. Or at least for her good, since he rarely gave her a second glance. Of course he flirted, but she knew this was how he was with everyone, how he charmed his way through life.

Jake had that air about him that invited her to admire, adore and desire him, while making it perfectly clear that the rest of him was off limits. So, even if she were allowed close enough to touch, there would be a part of his heart she could never reach.

But Maya was absolutely, completely and utterly in love with him. And even though she believed, totally and unequivocally, that this was a man who would never fall in love with her, she still held onto a small thread of hope that it was possible. Just as people buy lottery tickets every week, Maya knew that, although her odds of success were very small indeed, it wasn't altogether impossible that one day Jake might be hers. And until then she contented herself with fantasising about their possible life together.

Sometimes Maya overheard Jake chatting on his mobile, waiting for his takeaway cappuccino, and she eavesdropped on the ups and downs of his love life. Maya listened to Jake juggle girlfriends, catching them in each hand, hiding one behind his back. And with every fresh revelation Maya's fears about Jake were etched more deeply. Yet she told herself that one day, when he fell in love with the right woman, he might stop all that. And Maya thought maybe, with a little luck and a lot of wishing, she could be that woman.

The bell above the door rang. Maya glanced up as Jake walked in. He shook the water off his umbrella and instantly flicked on a dazzling smile. Maya sat up straight and sucked in her stomach. Jake walked over to the counter, still flashing his thousand-kilowatt grin.

'I'll have…' he began.

'Medium cappuccino, extra chocolate beans,' Maya finished.

'That's right. Thanks.'

Maya turned away to the coffee machine, wishing she'd washed her hair that morning.

'It's quieter than usual today,' Jake said.

'I know,' Maya squeaked, again worrying about the ever-diminishing amount of customers and her rather precarious financial situation.

Jake said nothing and the echo of Maya's voice sounded shrill in the silence. She wracked her brains for something devastatingly witty to say, but her mind went blank. Finally Maya turned back to him, handing over the coffee. Jake slipped off the lid and sipped it. 'Perfect.'

'You must have asbestos lips.' Maya smiled, gazing at them.

He handed her a fiver. 'Sorry?'

'No, I mean,' Maya said, 'I only meant, I... I can't drink it so hot.'

'Oh?'

'Yes, but I didn't mean to...'

Maya searched for the words, losing herself in Jake's perfect features. Just then his phone rang and he turned to answer it, walking away as he spoke. Maya watched him leave, leaning a little to catch the view. She waited until the door closed behind him, then groaned and banged her head softly against the counter.

Maya hadn't always felt so frustrated. Although she could barely remember it, twenty years ago she'd been supremely happy. Free from doubt and fear, she'd known exactly what she wanted from life and just how to get it. Desire and direction were joined in her, and her future was certain to be wonderful.

As a child Maya often imagined the glorious life she'd have as a grown-up, with a beautiful man who adored her, a child of her own and work she enjoyed as much as play.

Maya had liked to chat about these things with God. She hadn't been raised religiously, so it wasn't a specific god she talked to. It was more of a feeling she connected with, a feeling that someone or something was out there. Listening.

Often Maya directed her dreams at the sky, the clouds, or a bird, or a tree. In everything she saw she felt the vibration of magic, of cosmic energies, of God. So she talked and talked. And, even though she didn't hear answers in her head, she knew they came because she felt them in her heart.

It thrilled Maya to chat like this, feeling as though she was harbouring a special, secret connection with creation. She skipped along the pavement, leaping up to touch the branches of trees, catching sunlight in her hands and grinning as her heart tingled with joy. Maya didn't mind when people gave her funny looks. She just smiled, wanting to share her secret with them but not quite knowing how.

Maya engaged with the world as though it was a living, breathing being she loved, imagining she was completely connected with everything, part of it body and soul. She looked for patterns in the rhythms of life, searching for hints and clues while pondering the questions life gave her. She played with everything she saw, twirling with leaves as they danced in the wind, imagining them blown by the breath of a universe that delighted in everything it created.

Sometimes Maya was silent, spending long, languid moments just staring at things. She loved being outside, sitting on the grass and gazing up at swallows dipping in the sky. But her favourite experience above all was watching frogs. Maya liked to lie on her stomach, waiting for a quiet rustling in the grass. And when a tiny green frog jumped past her nose, her heart leapt with it. She'd creep up close after they landed and watch their tiny hearts pumping while they waited for the next urge to leap.

Lily had often watched Maya chatting away to the sky and it had worried her. But she'd told herself Maya would grow out of it. And so she did. One day Maya just stopped talking with God.

She was nine years old. The first day at her new school. She had been so excited to meet new friends, to take them on her walks, to share her secrets with them all. But that first afternoon, as Maya skipped past the trees and talked to the birds, she learnt the horror of being the odd one out, of being mocked in the playground. Their taunting voices filled the air and tears fell down her face. The humiliation slid down her spine, crept into her chest and muffled her heart. The sour taste stayed in her mouth for days and the voices haunted her dreams for years.

That was the last time she looked up at the sky, smiled at nothing and talked to something she only sensed but couldn't see. Later in life Maya still remembered that moment and understood why most adults walked through life so carefully contained, too scared to smile at strangers. She understood that the fear of embarrassment is a great dampener of joy.

Now Maya no longer shared her heart with God, or with anyone else. She kept her desires and dreams to herself. Secrets locked away, only to be studied in moments of great solitude.

But the fact that she no longer admitted them to anyone didn't stop her dreaming all day long. Her desires lingered in her mind while she leant on the counter at the café. And, as long as no one interrupted her, Maya could daydream for hours.

Maya sat behind the till digesting a sandwich and another cupcake, the disappointment with Jake having sent her back again to the comfort of chocolate. She flicked through a magazine, enviously eyeing up the skinny celebrities and trying to forget that it was barely midday and she'd already broken her no-chocolate promise, twice.

Maya tried hard not to think about Jake; instead she decided to focus on cleaning the coffee machine. It didn't look like she'd get many customers that morning, so she took the opportunity to take it apart.

Maya, her head still deep in the coffee machine, was interrupted by a series of little coughs. She turned to see a tiny old lady standing on the other side of the counter.

'Oh, hello.' Maya quickly wiped her hands on her apron. 'I was just…'

'I'd like a large hot chocolate, dear,' the old lady declared, 'with lots of froth.'

'Oh, I'm sorry, I can't. I'm in the middle of cleaning the machine.'

Maya braced herself for the old lady to get annoyed. But she only laughed, then pressed her tiny nose to the display case and pointed to the chocolate-chip and orange cake Maya had baked that morning.

'Well then, dear, I'll have a large slice of that delicious-looking cake instead.'

Maya nodded and opened the case, pulling it out. She cut a slice while the old lady watched her with a smile. Maya tried to keep her head down and focus. But there was something about this woman, Maya realised, that made her smile too. She couldn't put her finger on it, but there was something special about her.

'Would you like to join me?' the old lady asked.

'Sorry?'

'For a slice of cake.'

'Oh, I don't… I'm a little busy.'

The old lady looked at her. 'Are you?'

Maya frowned. Customers never spoke to her so directly, if at all. With the exception of several scattered thank-yous, nothing of significance ever occurred in her café interactions.

Maya eyed the old lady suspiciously. For such a forthright person she appeared deceptively meek.

A tiny woman with a short grey bob, blue twinset, pearls and little eyes that stared out intently behind gold-rimmed glasses. But her eyes sparkled. For no reason, or perhaps for this very reason, Maya suddenly trusted her.

'No, I'm not busy,' she admitted.

'So why don't you join me?'

This was something Maya hadn't done since she was a little girl. In those days she chatted with everyone, constantly sharing slices of cakes, flapjacks and cups of hot chocolate with customers. And now she realised just how much she'd missed it. With a slight ache in her heart Maya nodded, walked round the counter and followed the old lady to a table.

'I'm Rose,' she said, sitting down.

'Maya.'

They sat in silence. Rose delicately devoured her cake. After several mouthfuls she looked up.

'I was right. This is absolutely delicious.'

'Thank you.'

'Don't you want any?'

'I don't eat cake,' Maya lied.

'Oh,' Rose said, with a little smile.

Maya sat back in her chair, trying to ignore the lure of the cake, resisting the urge to snatch it from Rose and stuff it into her own mouth.

As Rose finished the last few crumbs, carefully picking them off her plate with a moist finger, she regarded the young woman carefully. Maya shifted uneasily in her seat. She wasn't used to being looked into like that and it made her uncomfortable.

'You're not often here, are you?' Rose said softly.

'Every day except Sunday,' Maya said.

'That's not what I meant, dear.'

'Oh?'

'I mean, you don't appear to be really living your life, but rather watching it being lived,' Rose said. 'And that's why you feel so… unfulfilled.'

'Unfulfilled?' Maya frowned.

'Aren't you? I'm sorry, dear, but you seem rather unfulfilled to me.'

Maya was both shocked and touched that the old lady spoke with such honesty. And when she said 'dear' she seemed to really mean it. As Maya smiled Rose returned it with a look of such compassion that to her great surprise and embarrassment, tears came to Maya's eyes.

'Yes, I am. Deeply.'

'You can't hide it.' Rose nodded. 'It's all in the eyes.'

'What's wrong with my eyes?' Maya asked.

'Your eyes, my dear, have a distinct lack of sparkle.'

Maya and Rose now had a plate of chocolate flapjacks on the table between them. The old lady munched on her third while the young woman watched her. Rose nudged the plate across the table, but Maya shook her head.

'Are you sure you don't want one?' Rose asked, crumbs falling onto her lap. 'They're quite delicious.'

'I know. I've eaten at least a hundred this year,' Maya said, unwrapping this semi-truth carefully, revealing a little piece of herself to Rose.

'Oh, but that's not too many,' Rose said.

'Yes, well, I wasn't really telling the truth,' Maya admitted. 'I eat at least three a day.'

Rose smiled, popped the last piece of flapjack into her mouth and chewed with relish.

'How do you do it?' Maya asked. 'How do you eat so much and stay so thin?'

'If I told you, you wouldn't believe me.'

'Why not?' Maya frowned, trying to imagine what spectacular weight-loss secret this old lady could possibly be concealing.

'I can't tell you now.' Rose brushed crumbs from her lap. 'You're on a journey, and you'll get there. But there are things you must experience in life before you discover the secret to always being your perfect weight.'

'You know it –' Maya was horrified. '– And you're not going to tell me?'

'Life is like any other education,' Rose explained. 'You've got to grasp the basic principles first before you graduate to the higher truths. If I told you right away, you wouldn't know what to do with them. And, more importantly, you wouldn't believe me.'

Maya eyeballed the old lady indignantly, suddenly furious, wanting to choke these truths out of her if she had to. Finally, as the anger and frustration swelled up inside her, ready to burst out, Maya sighed, realising Rose was right.

'I don't even know how to achieve the simple things in life,' Maya said. 'Love, success and happiness seem so completely impossible to me. People live them every day, but I can't. I don't know what's wrong with me.'

'Ah.' Rose discreetly patted her hair, catching a stray curl and putting it into place. 'Now I see what your first lesson needs to be.'

Maya sat up a little, trying not to look too intrigued. For all her general cynicism, she realised that, if some people held the secrets to life, Rose was one of them. She'd never met anyone so happy, so quietly content with life.

'Before you try to get everything you want,' Rose said, 'start to notice how hard you are on yourself. This is the beginning. You need to start being more gentle.'

'What do you mean?'

Maya leant forward and Rose reached out to gently pat her hand. Warmth flushed Maya's skin and, just as she was about to pull away, she realised she hadn't been touched so tenderly in a long time. Indeed it'd been quite some time since she'd been touched at all.

'My dear,' Rose said, 'you think there's something wrong with you. You think you're overweight, that you're inadequate and have no willpower. But it's not true. You hate working in this café, and you think you're a coward for not following your real dreams. But you're not. You wish you had a boyfriend, partly because you're lonely, but mostly because you believe that not having one means you're unlovable. Nothing could be further from the truth.'

Rose leant closer, fixing her sparkling green eyes on Maya, who couldn't help but smile a little, although she wanted to cry.

'How do you know all this about me?'

'I'm an old woman. I know a lot of things. And when you start paying attention to other people, you'll notice all kinds of things you never saw before. Most people are too busy worrying about themselves to pay anybody else much notice.' Rose sighed a little, then smiled. 'It's a shame, because they miss so much.'

'I almost missed you.'

'Yes, my dear, you almost did.'

Maya smiled again. There was something about this woman that made it hard not to smile. She seemed so content, so pleased with everything, and her happiness was infectious. Maya wasn't a touchy-feely person, but all of sudden she just wanted to reach over to Rose and hug her.

Rose grinned, as though she knew what Maya was thinking. Maya glanced out of the window, embarrassed. It had stopped raining. She hoped this wouldn't mean a sudden rush of customers. For, while she needed the income, she wanted to keep talking to Rose even more. Maya's gaze returned to the old lady.

'Why are you looking at me like that?'

'I'm sorry, dear, looking at you like what?'

'As though you know something about me that I don't.'

'Oh, you know it. You just refuse to believe it.'

'Believe what?'

'That you're absolutely perfect,' Rose smiled, 'exactly as you are: single and struggling and so... sexy. If you only believed that, then your life would begin to unfold into something magnificent.'

This idea was so radical to Maya, such a shock to her system, that she barely even heard Rose say it.

'No,' she said. 'If Jake fell in love with me; if I wrote a bestseller and lost a stone. Then my life would be perfect.'

Rose raised her eyebrows, and her green eyes shone. How she wished she could tell the young woman all the secrets to a happy life right now. It would save so much time, so much pain. But there was nothing she could do about it. This wasn't how it was done. Because it never worked.

Rose knew from experience that while inspired instructions were essential on the path to fulfilment and joy, alone they were never enough. For some reason, that even she didn't quite understand, advice had to be balanced with experience before such instructions were written on the heart instead of simply held in the head.

'You're trying to graduate before you've learnt your lessons,' Rose said, trying to set Maya in the right direction.

'But I've been waiting for that life forever,' Maya complained. 'I don't think I can bear to wait any longer.'

'Oh, my dear, don't worry about that. People fall in love in a second, book deals are made in a day and people have lost ten pounds in a week,' Rose said, trying to drop little clues into the conversation, like hot toffee dropped into cold water. 'But it's much better if we don't get the things we *really* want until we've learnt our life's lessons.'

'Lessons about what?' Maya asked, curious and hopeful that perhaps the old lady was about to tell her the longed-for secrets after all.

'Life gives everyone challenges, difficult situations they think they don't want. Conditions like being lonely, broke and overweight. But people push against these things so strongly that they miss the gifts hidden inside them.'

'Gifts?' Maya asked, incredulous.

Rose knew then that her first instinct had been correct. She couldn't tell Maya all the secrets to life right now, because she simply wouldn't believe them. And that would be no use at all. Maya's cynicism overpowered everything else: her desire, her curiosity, her longing for a happier life. She was dipped in it, head to toe, and its mixture of mistrust and resignation fogged her mind and gave off little puffs of suspicion-smoke that clouded her vision.

Rose wasn't in the business of trying to convince anyone of anything, but she saw a real sweetness in this young woman and, for that, decided to try. She also noticed, deep inside Maya's exhausted eyes, soft sparks of hope, buried under years of sadness and disappointment but still desperately trying to shine through. It was this hope that Rose had to awaken first, if Maya stood any chance at happiness at all.

'Well, if you look deep into these situations, these seeming twists of fate, if you look for the secrets to happiness contained within them, then you would sense both how to transcend them,' Rose explained, 'and how to be happy along the way.'

Maya considered this carefully. 'But I don't see how the condition of being broke or overweight could contain any secrets to happiness. Wouldn't I be happier if those things just changed? If I was rich and thin, I'd be happy. I think that's all there is to it.'

'Well, it all depends on how you get there,' Rose said, knowing that this was the truth most people had the hardest time understanding. 'People who attain great wealth, even by doing what they love, usually aren't completely happy if they didn't follow the right route getting there.'

'I don't think I understand,' Maya said. But her curiosity grew, she wanted to be told the secrets she suspected this woman could give her, clues to contentment she'd known as a child but could no longer remember.

'Some people have everything you want, but it doesn't make them truly happy,' Rose said. 'That's because they sped down the path without looking. They were so focused on their goal that they missed the realisations about real joy, and surrender, the opportunities for compassion and, most of all, the experiences that could crack open their hearts and connect them to God.'

Maya sat in silence for a moment, rather awed by what had just been said. Rose smiled softly, seeing how her words were beginning to reignite the sparkle in Maya's eyes.

'So, how do I get what I want?' Maya asked. 'Without missing those things?'

'Well, dear, these lessons are different for everyone. We each hold unseen gifts that need expressing; we each hide unique wounds that need healing,' Rose said. 'If we walk our paths, listening to other people's instructions and our own intuition, life will give us what we need.'

'Really? Is that always the case?' Maya, having felt nothing but stuck for the last ten years, couldn't quite believe this.

'Yes,' Rose replied, with a smile. 'Your life is so full of potentially glorious lessons and gifts right now I'm surprised you're not tripping over every second step you take.'

'Well, I am rather clumsy.' Maya laughed. 'How did you know?'

Rose's eyes shone mischievously. 'You're constantly being offered lessons to learn and gifts to gather. But if you ignore the nudges you'll soon find yourself hit over the head. Indeed, if you insist on ignoring them for too much longer I'd start to watch out for falling bricks while you're walking down the street.'

A horrified look passed across Maya's face.

'What are they, these lessons and gifts? Can you tell me?'

The young woman looked across the table with such a sense of expectation, and spoke with such hope in her voice that, no matter what the rules and regulations were, Rose couldn't possibly say no.

'Compassion. Courage. Connection,' she said.

'Oh, I see,' Maya said, although she didn't really see at all. Still, it was a good start.

'Those are your keys. They will unlock the happiness that waits inside you.' Rose smiled at the image of Maya as a little treasure chest, waiting to be unlocked. 'Without these keys you might grab onto the things you want in the world, but you'll still feel uneasy and scared of losing them. Your heart will be cut off from your senses. You'll have everything, but you might feel nothing at all.'

'No,' Maya said quickly. 'I don't want that.'

'That's why it's much better to create your dreams carefully, rather than rushing headlong into them, or having them fall into your lap. The magic of manifestation is all very well and good,' Rose warned, 'but experiences like compassion, courage and connection are essential to living a joyous life. Without these you would feel lost, but you wouldn't know why. You could have love, wealth and beauty, but you still wouldn't be truly happy.'

As Maya listened Rose adjusted herself in the chair, tweaking her twinset and perfecting her pearls.

'I know you might not want to hear it, dear,' Rose said gently, 'but your first lesson, before you do anything else, is to realise that there is nothing wrong with you. To see that you're absolutely perfect, exactly as you are. This is compassion.'

Maya closed her eyes, sighing softly.

'That is the first, and most important, reason you don't yet have the life you want,' Rose explained. 'Because truly, deep down, you don't believe you deserve it. You think you're not good enough.'

Maya swallowed back her tears.

'Try saying it,' Rose suggested. 'Try saying that you deserve to have everything you want.'

Maya opened her mouth. Words formed and hovered on her tongue, waiting for her to speak. But she couldn't.

'I don't know why I find it so hard.'

'It's okay. Just try again. But this time, say it even if you don't feel it.'

Maya took a long, deep breath, summoning the words from down inside in her belly. 'I deserve to have a loving relationship. I deserve to write and sell a wonderful book. I deserve to have a beautiful body.'

Maya exhaled in a rush. Rose gave her hand a little squeeze across the table.

'Well done, dear. So how do you feel?'

Maya shook her head and shrugged. 'Undeserving and guilty, but I don't understand it. I suppose I think… why should I get the things I want? What makes me so special?'

'Exactly!' Rose exclaimed suddenly, slapping her tiny hand on the table so hard that Maya jumped. 'That's what most people think. And it's so sad because it keeps them from having the things they long for in life.'

Maya nodded. She was slowly beginning to understand what Rose was trying to show her. She had never noticed it before: the weight of guilt that sat on her chest like a shiny black stone. Now it was all she could feel. And it was so heavy she could barely breathe.

'Listen,' Rose said, leaning forward, her eyes shining, conspiratorial, full of secrets. 'You can't battle these negative beliefs, because they're very powerful and shared by most of the world. But you can bypass them.'

'Really? Are you sure?' Maya asked, still struggling to breathe properly, and wondering just how long she'd felt like this.

'Absolutely, you just have to be practical. Don't think about whether or not you deserve to be happy,' Rose said. 'Know instead that you *need* to be happy, for the benefit of the rest of the world.'

'What do you mean?'

'Everyone on this planet needs to be happy. It isn't a selfish impulse. They owe it to the rest of humanity.'

'They do?'

'Yes,' Rose said. 'When you're happy you light up those around you and make the world a better place to be. But when you're unhappy you spread unhappiness. You may not want to, but you can't help it. Your sadness just seeps out and into those around you. And there's nothing you can do to stop it.'

Maya nodded. This she understood.

'In order to light up the world, you need to make yourself happy first.'

Maya was silent.

'Don't you want that?' Rose asked.

Maya nodded reluctantly, barely able to admit it. Tears gathered again, and her breath held in her throat. The old woman gazed at Maya until she started to cry. Then, slowly and quietly, Rose moved to sit next to her. Maya wept while Rose held her, hugging and rocking her gently.

'You just need to forgive yourself,' Rose whispered. 'That's all. For everything you've ever done. Because the only way to stop hurting other people is to stop hurting yourself.'

As the truth of these words sank in, Maya sobbed. For all the pain she'd ever caused others and all the pain she'd ever caused herself. The times she'd yelled at her mother because she wanted to go out and play instead of stay and serve, the cruel words she'd sometimes screamed and lies she'd told. These memories, scattered among many more, built up and released themselves in Maya's sobs.

Most of all, Maya cried for the millions upon millions of times she'd been horrible to herself. For all the little put-downs, the cutting criticisms, for every time she'd looked in the mirror and hated what she saw.

Rose hugged her. She stroked Maya's hair and told her everything would be all right, that we all hurt people, but we're all innocent in our pain. Because, if we could possibly behave any better, if we could find love in our hearts instead of hate, we would.

Gradually, ever so softly, Maya's tears washed away her guilt. Eventually she breathed deeply, wiped her eyes and looked up at Rose.

'I haven't cried like that in a really long time. No one has held me like that since…'

'I know, dear,' Rose said softly, 'I know.'

Rose stood on the doorstep and Maya leant against the door, reluctant to see her go. The old woman reached out and Maya squeezed her hand tightly.

'You're going to be fine.' Rose chuckled. 'In fact, you're going to be wonderful. This is the first step in your journey. You've started to open your heart. Now you can begin to see the truth of who you really are.'

Maya grinned, letting go of Rose's hand as she stepped onto the pavement. She watched the old lady walk away until she turned at the end of the road and waved. Maya grinned and waved back, feeling lighter and brighter than she had in a very, very long time.

*E*venings were usually the same for Maya. She shut the café at six, prepared things for the next day; then walked over to Flicks, her local video shop, to find a film to lose herself in. In addition to chocolate and daydreaming, films were Maya's other drug of choice when it came to numbing herself to the pains of life. She went to this particular video shop because of Tim, the assistant, who would chat and flirt with her while she picked out that night's rental.

Maya wasn't really attracted to Tim, regarding him as a friend rather than a potential boyfriend, although the flirtation was always a welcome and much-needed boost to her flagging ego. Tim had a way of making Maya feel beautiful and desirable, no matter how she felt about herself. The way he looked at her, with surreptitious glances of admiration, the way he spoke to her, kindly and with great interest, always made Maya feel better. Indeed, Jake's visits to the café aside, seeing Tim was the highlight of Maya's day.

Occasionally, in moments of great loneliness, Maya considered giving Tim a try. But then, with great restraint, she'd hold back, suspecting that he cared about her and not wanting to hurt him.

Maya gave Tim cakes in exchange for rentals, watching his reactions carefully to learn his favourites. He always said he loved them all, but Maya could tell when he really meant it. After they'd said goodbye Maya would return to her flat to sit on the sofa and lose herself in a film, while slowly but steadily working her way through a tub of cinder-toffee ice cream drowned in chocolate sauce.

But this evening was different. Maya didn't feel like watching a film. She was too excited by the life all around her to bother with fiction. For the first time in years she didn't want to dream; she wanted to feel.

So Maya stepped out of the café and just kept walking. The soft September air blew gently across her skin. Maya realised the weather had been like this for a few weeks, but until now she hadn't noticed the soft sensations of ambling through a late summer evening. Now Maya saw how the light fell at magic hour, how the sun touched her skin, so she almost felt held. She closed her eyes as the breeze blew, playing with her, inviting her to move, to dance.

Maya grinned, suddenly filled with joy, as though she had just uncovered a particularly beautiful secret she'd always hoped was true.

At the end of the road Maya turned towards the park. Leafy trees lined its edges, clusters of wild flowers struggled for space on the ground. Maya stepped through the overgrown grasses, realising she couldn't remember the last time she'd been in nature. When she reached an old oak tree she found a soft place to sit and snuggled down.

The park was empty. The air was still. Maya sank into a deep peace. Her mind was silent and her heart was full. As she sat, simply breathing, she conjured up Rose in her mind, wanting to remember, to feel her still there.

Magical things never happened to Maya, yet here it was. She remembered she'd rejected Rose at first and, if the old woman hadn't been so persistent, she would have missed the experience altogether. It occurred to Maya then that if she glanced up a little more often, if she actually started to look people in the eye, there might be a whole lot more magic out there waiting for her.

In the silence Maya became acutely aware of the stillness inside and all around her. She knew then that this was true life, and all the drama and noise on top of it was just caused by people desperately longing for peace but not knowing where to find it.

Maya laughed at the absurd, seemingly impossible, simplicity of it all. And as her laughter drifted away into the air she heard a voice, words that seemed to come from her soul.

'*The miracles of life are everywhere,*' it said. '*Sometimes you just need to take a closer look.*'

Maya smiled, leaning back against the tree, sometimes softly humming, sometimes silent, until the sun went down.

As Maya stepped into her flat, Doughnut, her cat, ran up, winding through her legs and purring. Maya giggled and Doughnut looked up with surprise. It wasn't often Maya laughed like that.

Maya knelt down to pick up the cat and walked into the kitchen.

'Were you worried about me, fatty? Did you think I got lost?'

She popped Doughnut down on the counter and opened the cupboards to look for tuna.

'Well, you were right,' Maya chatted as the cat looked up at her. 'I did. I was really lost. And now I'm finally starting to feel found again.'

Maya put the plate of tuna on the floor and watched Doughnut tuck into her dinner. 'You don't know what I'm talking about, do you? You've got contentment and satisfaction hard-wired into you.'

Maya glanced past Doughnut's swishing tail to the cookie jar. This was normally her first port of call: a couple of chocolate biscuits, a few slices of bread, before she started on the ice cream. She usually ate the biscuits while toasting the bread, munching as she walked through the flat, undressing on her way to the bedroom to change into baggy bedclothes.

Maya always slipped her oversized pyjamas on with some relief. She was no longer on display. She could sink into the sofa, hiding little rolls of fat under bagginess, and keep eating without feeling she would burst out of her clothes. Of course this trickery didn't really work and, deep down, Maya still felt as disappointed with her body as if she'd been trying to squeeze into tight leather hot-pants.

Maya glanced at the curve of her belly, then back at the cookie jar, relieved, and rather surprised, to discover that she didn't actually feel like eating. She wasn't even particularly hungry, despite not having eaten since lunchtime. But it was more than that. She felt full. Not of food but of something else: a sense of contentment, of joy. Excited emotions bubbled up inside her, and there wasn't much room for food on top of all that.

Maya grinned, absolutely thrilled. She felt at the start of some great adventure. She didn't know what would happen next. She didn't know what she'd do. It was as though all those feelings she'd been suppressing with food suddenly had free rein.

And, much to Maya's surprise and delight, she didn't feel about to be overwhelmed with pain. It was as though Rose had purged her of all that, to reveal her excitement, her passion, her joy. Maya twirled in the kitchen and laughed.

The phone rang. Doughnut, licking up the last of her tuna, looked up. Maya stopped spinning. It was quite late, and she didn't get many calls. For a second Maya thought that by some miracle it might be Jake, finally calling to ask her out. But she told herself not to be so *stupid*, since he didn't even have her number.

'Oh,' Maya said, realising she'd just criticised herself. Usually this slip was so normal she wouldn't have noticed it. But, with her new-found compassion, the word felt out of place.

'I'm sorry,' Maya apologised to herself as she picked up the phone.

It was her kooky cousin, Faith.

'Hey, May,' Faith said, as she always did. 'Are you sitting down?'

'No, should I be?'

'Yes. Absolutely.'

Maya didn't move. 'Okay, I am.'

'No, you're not.'

Maya frowned. 'How do you know?'

'I've just seen a psychic. My sixth sense is primed.'

Maya laughed and sat on the sofa.

'Okay. So?'

'So, it was absolutely amazing.'

Maya smiled, not at all surprised.

'No,' Faith said, hearing her smile, 'this time was different. This woman is the real deal.'

Faith was forever going to psychics, healers, palm-readers and astrologers. These things fascinated her. But Maya had never believed in them and, although she'd never tell Faith, really thought they were a con. If Maya believed in anything it was psychology, theory, analysis: anything she could read proof of and make sense of in her mind. But she still listened to Faith talk about them, and had even let herself be dragged to an astrologer once, but only because she loved Faith and wanted to be supportive.

Faith also had nothing. No man. No cash. No reasonable hope of things ever being any different. But, for some strange reason, she'd always been a lot happier about it than Maya.

'So, tell me about...'

'Sophie.'

'That's a funny name for a psychic.'

'What did you expect? Crystal?'

'I suppose it'd be more fitting.' Maya smiled.

'Shut up,' Faith said. 'I saw her yesterday and she was simply amazing. She told me things even

I didn't know about me. And silly little facts she couldn't possibly know.'

'Like what?'

'Like the time Phoenix and I went to that Goddess workshop in Glastonbury.'

'The one where you danced naked round a bonfire?'

'Yep, that one.'

They both laughed.

'But it was more than that, she just seemed to *know*.'

'Know what?'

'Everything. Being with her was a transcendental experience. Her energy was simply amazing, as though she'd unlocked all the secrets of the universe and held them in her heart.'

Maya smiled, suddenly intrigued.

'She was so calm, so content. I don't think I've ever met a happier person in my life. And she said I had the potential to be like that too.'

'Really?'

'Yeah, well, she said we all do. She told me there was this moment in her life, standing on a mountain in the Arizona desert, that she realised it.'

'Realised what?'

'That we create our own lives.' Faith focused on remembering Sophie's words. 'It was at dawn, on her twenty-first birthday. The desert was silent and empty. As the sun came up she buzzed with the energy of everything surrounding her. And she felt a supreme sense of connection with it all, and with God. Then she heard a voice.'

'Really?' Maya shivered. 'What did it say?'

'Hold on, I wrote it down.'

Maya waited while Faith rustled around.

'Okay,' Faith began. 'It said: no matter what's happened in your past, you have two lives to choose from now. One is a life where you're disconnected from the world, out of control and at the mercy of your circumstances. You're pessimistic about life and fearful of what might happen next. You want things but don't know how to get them. And, even if you have a lot, you still feel lonely, with a longing at the centre of your soul.'

Maya sighed, tears in her eyes. She knew this way of being only too well. She'd lived it for most of her life.

Faith sensed her sadness. 'It's okay,' she said. 'It gets better.'

'That's a relief.'

'In the other one,' Faith went on, 'even with life's knocks, you retain a sense of connectedness with your self and your source. You understand the rhythms of life. You have everything you want and exactly what you need. You feel joy, excitement and optimism, and look forward to what could happen next. Underneath it all you feel content. You feel complete.'

Maya sighed happily. This reminded her of Rose. Maya knew that if she hadn't met the old lady that morning she probably wouldn't be listening to what Faith was telling her now.

'So, how do I do it?' Maya asked. 'How do I live that way?'

'Perhaps you should see Sophie.'

'Yeah, nice try.'

'Seriously,' Faith said, 'I can't explain it. You have to experience it. You have to see her.'

'What else did she say?'

'That at any time you can create joy within you. It's always available. We knew it once; we felt it, we laughed it, we lived it, before we lost it to the fear and doubt that surrounded us,' Faith said, having memorised every word. 'And the opportunity to feel it again waits within every moment, within everyone. Just as it waits for you.'

Maya was silent, then sighed.

'But it's not so easy just to live like that, is it? I mean, I wish I had a man who...'

'You mean Jake?' Faith interrupted. 'Okay, let me tell you something Sophie said to me. She told me I'll fall in love many times in my life, and I might never settle down, but I shouldn't worry about it. If I embrace love, without trying to fit into society's expectations, then I'll be truly happy.'

'That's a nice idea,' Maya considered. 'But doesn't it bother you, that you might never have a lifelong relationship?'

'You know, I actually find it liberating, to let go of trying to create the ultimate fairytale. It's a relief. To stop trying to catch men, trap them and change them. Now I can let go of all that and just love them.'

Maya sighed deeply, briefly bathing herself in the glory of this possibility.

'Sophie said I have the potential to connect with the source of universal love, with the current of life, and when I do I'll feel more loved than I've ever felt in my life. Then I'll finally be free,' Faith smiled. 'Hey, I think I'll go to Arizona too. You could come with me. It'd be fantastic!'

'I wish I could be free.' Maya sighed again, ignoring Faith's wild idea. 'I mean, I want a relationship that'll last forever. But I wish I could be free of needing it.'

'I know. That's exactly how I felt.'

'I wish I could let go of my complete obsession with Jake. And not just that; I'm truly fed up with the café. I barely make a living…'

'That's because your heart isn't in it.'

'I know, and I want to do something where my heart *is* in it. I want to write.'

'You can write,' Faith said, wishing her cousin would seize the day once in a while. 'Write when you've got no customers, write when you finish work.'

Doughnut jumped onto Maya's lap and snuggled against her.

'I know. I know I should. But I'm too grumpy. I couldn't write anything inspirational in this condition.'

'So you sit at home consoling yourself with chocolate cake and ice cream, and go to bed feeling disappointed with yourself and your life,' Faith said.

'Yes,' Maya admitted.

'You really should see her.'

'I don't know.'

Maya didn't want to get duped into another crazy experience. But something inside her had shifted. Rose had opened her up a little, making her curious about things she'd previously dismissed.

'If she can help, shouldn't you give it a try?' Faith pressed her. 'You don't have to believe in it all. Sophie is amazing, whether you believe in her or not. And, anyway, what's a hundred and fifty quid in the grand scheme of things?'

'A hundred and fifty pounds! Are you serious?'

'Hey. It's nothing. How do you expect Jake to fall for you if you don't think you're worth a hundred and fifty quid? Don't you deserve even that kind of investment?'

If Faith hadn't used that word, things might have gone differently. But what Rose had said to Maya about believing she deserved what she wanted had stuck with her. And if Sophie could indeed help her be happier, then she owed it to her customers, to Faith, to those all around her, to try.

'Maybe…' Maya said, wavering.

'Excellent, I'll make an appointment.'

'Wait a second. I want to think about it.'

But it was too late. Faith had already hung up.

It was the first of October. The day before Maya's appointment with the psychic. The memory of Rose had faded, and it seemed to Maya that life was back to its normal routine. Except for one thing. Maya felt a little different, although she couldn't quite put her finger on how.

That lunchtime, just as she was succumbing to a slice of apricot frangipane and fifteen chocolate truffles, Maya realised what it was she felt. Hope. She felt hopeful. That little buzzing in her stomach was hope. Rose had affected her after all. The optimism she'd spoken of, the openness, was a part of Maya now and, luckily for her, she couldn't quite shift it.

This bothered Maya, because she already knew what followed hope: disappointment. And she'd had enough disappointment to last a lifetime. So she told herself to snap out of it, because her waistline really couldn't handle another disappointment-induced frangipane feast.

In a bid to save her belly Maya tried to squash her hope. She fixed her gaze on the few remaining truffles and focused on the ache of guilt and self-loathing she felt for having eaten so many. Within seconds Maya squashed her hope and felt awful, helpless and full of self-loathing. She sighed, wiped the counter and walked over to the pile of dirty plates in the sink.

But, to her surprise, by the time she was rearranging the sugar bowls the hope was back. And no amount of self-criticism worked to get rid of it.

In the end Maya left it alone, bobbing up and down inside her, and got on with her day. Which was lucky, because tomorrow her life would change forever.

Maya walked slowly down the street, trying to postpone the moment a little longer. She saw the destination just ahead and glanced down at Faith's instructions.

Maya stopped, for a second considering turning back. But she knew she couldn't now; she was just too curious. The heart that Rose had helped was still open. Optimism bubbled up inside her, and there wasn't much she could do about it.

Maya reached the address on her map and glanced up. '*Sophie the Psychic*' was emblazoned across a bright purple sign swinging gently in the wind.

Maya frowned, feeling utterly ridiculous. This was the furthest she'd ever gone in her quest for happiness and she was rather embarrassed about it. She berated herself for being so desperate in her bid for love, wealth and the perfect body that she'd see a psychic.

Maya had been dipped in cynicism; she had grown up in it, argued its viewpoint most of her life, and it was hard to abandon. She stood on the doorstep and thought suddenly of her father. Maya hadn't grown up with him, but he'd played his own small part in her life. He was a thoughtful, introspective man; a university academic who frowned on anything involving faith rather than facts. He would have been horrified to see Maya now.

But, since it was unlikely Maya would ever see him again, and had absolutely no intention of ever mentioning it if she did, that wouldn't be much of a problem. The problem was the thoughts that started taunting her as soon as the door opened.

When Maya saw Sophie for the first time, all her worst cynical, judgmental, sceptical fears were realised. Sophie was dressed head to toe in flowing purple robes, a velvet vision against the violet doorframe. It was exactly what Maya expected from a kooky charlatan trying to trick gullible, desperate women into believing she could see their futures.

Sophie was also beautiful, with long curly brown hair, a sweet face and a voluptuous figure. But all Maya could see were those purple robes.

'Hello. Welcome.' Sophie's smile was bright, sincere and true. It helped put Maya at ease a little. Despite her embarrassment, she offered a small smile in return and mumbled her thanks.

When Maya stepped inside, things didn't improve. The house seemed to be a mail-order psychic's residence. Everything was bright: red walls, yellow walls, blue and green walls. Esoteric pictures added to the rainbow effect, fairy lights decorated the stairs and the too-sweet notes of a flute floated through the air.

Maya took off her shoes at the door and sank her feet into the plush maroon carpets. Whatever Sophie's taste, she certainly wasn't short of cash. Sophie walked upstairs and Maya followed, doubting the decision with every step.

As they entered Sophie's psychic parlour Maya noted, with surprise and relief, that it didn't present anything too outrageous. Maroon carpets gave way to cream, and red only returned in the velvet curtains framing large windows that overlooked the garden. Fairy lights shimmered in the corner, a variety of gems sat on the table. Fortunately there was no crystal ball.

Maya hesitated in the doorway, eyeing the two empty chairs at the table. Sophie sat down and waited. After a moment or two of hovering Maya joined her.

'Well then,' Sophie said brightly. 'Why don't you tell me why you're here?'

Maya shrank back. She'd expected some preliminary chit-chat about the weather, or the price of crystal balls, and didn't really know what to say. Actually, that was a lie. She knew exactly what to say but didn't want to say it. Sophie watched her patiently. She clearly wasn't one for small talk.

'Well, I… um,' Maya stumbled reluctantly. 'Okay, I'm here because I'm not exactly happy with the way my life is right now. My cousin, Faith, came to see you. And it sounded pretty wonderful, what you said to her. So I decided to come myself and see what you'd say to me.'

'Ah, and why aren't you happy?'

Maya shrugged, but Sophie just waited.

'Okay, well.' Maya shifted awkwardly in her seat. 'I want a boyfriend. I want to be a writer. I want to lose twenty pounds. And I want to see if any of that's in my future.'

'Well, we'll see what we see.' Sophie smiled. 'But I can't show you your future, because you create your own future. I'll only help you see yourself more clearly, so you'll know how to get what you want. Is that okay?'

Maya nodded excitedly. 'Yeah, that's perfect. You gave Faith advice on how to fulfil the possibilities in her future; I hoped you might give me that too.'

Sophie stood and walked across the room. She reached a cabinet covered with rows and rows of crystals in every different size, shape and colour. She studied them thoughtfully. Then closed her eyes, floated her palms over the crystals and picked one.

Maya eyed Sophie suspiciously as she returned to the table. She could see that what Sophie held in her hand was small and pink. It might not be a crystal ball, but it wasn't far off.

Sophie sat down. She looked at Maya closely, her dark brown eyes now wide and bright. Maya shifted uneasily, holding her breath, feeling perhaps Sophie was seeing more than Maya wanted her to. Then Sophie shut her eyes. Moments later she placed the crystal on the table and looked at Maya.

'Now,' she began, 'you needn't feel bad about what I see. Just because you have challenges in your life doesn't mean there's anything wrong with you.

We've all got things to overcome. It's your path and it's perfect.'

Maya nodded, a little nervous. Sophie looked at her closely, carefully considering her nature, slowly examining her past, studying her present, glancing at her future and finally coming to a conclusion.

'You'll discover happiness,' Sophie said, 'when you find the courage to stop living a safe life and start living a true one.'

Maya breathed deeply, both excited and scared by this revelation. It shocked her that Sophie had hit exactly on the two forces that drove her life: her fears and her dreams. She felt, almost for the first time in her life, as though she'd really been seen.

'What do you mean by *true*?' Maya asked softly.

'Living true to yourself means taking risks to create what you want, like being a writer, for example.'

Maya sat up straight, now ready to pay attention to every word.

'It's about not seeking love or approval from others, or success in the outside world,' Sophie said. 'To live true is to do something because it's in your heart and it needs to be expressed. So you don't worry about whether or not you'll be a great writer, because that's not the point. A person living true to themselves doesn't consider success or failure. They do it because it feels right. They do it because they must.'

Maya had never considered living so irrationally. To her the possibility of success was a vital consideration before doing anything. That was exactly what had stopped her writing in the past.

'If you live according to your rational thoughts, you'll always be trapped in a small, seemingly safe life. But if you live true, the world will open up to you. And then you won't need to try and guess the future, because you know that, whatever it is, it'll be a glorious adventure.' Sophie rubbed the pink crystal against her velvet sleeve, warming it up. 'When you follow your heart you allow miraculous possibilities to unfold.'

As Sophie's words sank slowly into Maya's mind

she realised that, scary though it was, she loved the idea of living like that. She was sick of making decisions based on what she thought might happen next, when she really had no clue. It only made her hold back from every possibility, always scared that something might go wrong. It was years of containment, contraction, fear and perpetual disappointment. It was more of a living death than a life.

'You could make it your mantra,' Sophie suggested. 'Don't live safe, live true.'

'Yes.' Maya grinned. 'That's wonderful.'

Sophie smiled. Then, suddenly, she became serious and leant forward in her chair.

'But there's one thing you must understand, before you can hope to get what you want from life.' She put a hand in each pocket and pulled out two crystals, one white and one black. 'Until you understand this, you'll always be taking one step forward and two steps back.'

Maya stared at her, anxious to know the answer to this.

'You have two forces inside you,' Sophie said softly, holding up the jet-black crystal. 'One is personified by your mind. It creates fear and doubt inside you, making you live by rationality, worry and guilt. It wants your life to be safe, routine, normal, stuck and dull. It wants an ordinary life. And, if you listen to it, it will lead you to all those things.'

'Oh.' Maya sighed, knowing full well the force that was driving her life at the moment.

'But,' Sophie said, holding up the bright white crystal, 'the other is personified by your heart. It creates peace and bliss within you, and fulfilment and satisfaction in your life. It wants everything for you: love, wealth and joy. It wants an extraordinary life. And, if you let it, it will lead you to those things.'

'Really?' Maya asked. 'How?'

'Have you never talked to your heart?' Sophie seemed surprised. 'You should try it; it's wonderful.' She smiled, releasing a deep sigh of satisfaction, as though remembering something particularly magical.

'So,' Sophie said. 'Which force are you listening to?'

Maya sighed and Sophie nodded.

Half an hour later Maya was sipping an odd-tasting but strangely comforting herbal tea concoction, and happily munching on home-made ginger biscuits. She'd already decided she liked Sophie immensely. This was icing on the cake.

Sophie sat on the sofa, sinking back into the cushions, dipping biscuits into her tea and continuing to dispense her wisdom. She'd now disrobed to reveal a very ordinary white T-shirt and jeans.

Maya was surprised to realise the wardrobe change disappointed her a little. The robes may have been a little clichéd, but they were certainly fun and, given their glory, absolutely fitting to the occasion.

Maya sat cross-legged on the plush carpet and, between sips and munches, looked up at Sophie to show she was paying attention.

'You can have everything you want,' Sophie was saying. 'But it's best to get those things in the right order.'

Maya remembered this was something Rose had touched upon and she was eager to get clarification on the idea. 'There's a right order?'

'Yes. Of course it depends on the person.' Sophie balanced a biscuit on top of her teacup and studied Maya for a second. 'I see that you need to fulfil your heart's desire with your work first, before you fall in love.'

'Why?' Maya asked, a little annoyed.

'Well, it's always best to feel fulfilled first, before finding a man. Then you'll know the value of yourself, and you'll hold the key to your own happiness. So you won't turn into a vulnerable, needy, emotional mess the minute you fall in love.'

'I see.' Maya sighed, knowing this scenario intimately.

'Now it's time to sing the song of your soul,' Sophie said. 'You are a writer; I see that. Your heart longs to express itself through words. But you don't write, do you?'

Maya shook her head.

'Because you fear it won't be magnificent.'

Maya stared at Sophie, open-mouthed, wondering again how someone who'd only just met her could know her so well.

'Well, you mustn't concern yourself with that; you must just write. And one day it will be. Magnificence lies within you. You just have to find the courage to uncover it.'

Maya gazed at Sophie and smiled. Those words filled her with a combination of peace and joy she'd felt somewhere before. She shut her eyes, trying to remember. It was that night in the university library: as bright as lightning and as light as air.

Suddenly Maya felt filled with a bright white light. It swept through her body and shone into every part of her. In that moment she loved herself completely, utterly and unconditionally. For an instant Maya was so happy she could die.

Then it was gone. She'd had another fearful thought. Self doubt had crept into her serenity. Its darkness glided into her mind, swept across her chest and shut out the light. What if Sophie was wrong? Worse still, what if she was lying? For, while she longed to believe Sophie, how could she know for sure?

When Maya glanced up again she saw Sophie sitting on the carpet right in front of her.

'Your head and heart are fighting within you.'

Maya nodded.

'I know how hard it is to ignore your fears,' Sophie said. 'But I beg you to try. Or you'll never express your magnificence. I know it takes courage, but, believe me, you have that courage.'

'I don't think I do,' Maya said softly.

'But, that's only your mind.' Sophie said. 'That's a fear, not a fact.'

'So, what should I do?'

'Be bold.'

Maya squinted at Sophie through tears, not really sure of what she'd heard. 'Bold?'

'Right now you're a bunny rabbit.' Sophie smiled. 'You need to be a bear.'

Maya raised an eyebrow. 'A bear?'

'A lion. An eagle. A wolf. Whatever works for you. To override your fears you have to be powerful. You have to focus completely on who you want to be. Seize upon any shred of courage and magnify it. Whip yourself up into a state of passionate frenzy and just go for it.' Sophie gripped Maya's hands tightly, and Maya felt energy surging through her as if she'd just plugged herself into a light socket. 'Keep yourself in that state. Ignore all dissenting and critical thoughts. Ignore other people's reactions and opinions, until you feel completely magnificent, fearless and spectacular. In that state you can achieve everything you want. I promise you.'

Maya shifted a little, still holding Sophie's hands, thinking about what a momentous but incredible challenge this would be.

'And, after that, it's not enough just to sit back and feel it,' Sophie said, reading her thoughts. 'A lot of people say positive focus is all you need to manifest what you want, but it's not enough just to believe in yourself. You must act on it. You must take courageous steps in the direction of your dreams.'

Maya swallowed nervously.

'So,' Sophie said, dropping Maya's hands and throwing her arms into the air, 'what's the boldest thing you could do today?'

Maya thought for a moment or two, then shrugged. 'I don't know.'

'Yes, you do!'

Again Sophie's energy surged through Maya, making her fingers tingle and her hair static.

'All right, I do!' Maya exclaimed, loving that Sophie was such a little firecracker. Her energy and enthusiasm for life were literally infectious.

'Okay. A couple of years ago I was ill,' Maya said. 'I had one of those horrible flu things when you're half unconscious most of the time. I shut the café; I lay in bed for a week. But when I was awake I wrote. It was incredible. I loved every single minute of it. I wasn't working, but I didn't feel guilty because

I couldn't have served a cup of coffee without fainting. I just wrote. And, in a little way, I felt what it must be like to be a full-time writer.'

Sophie laughed. 'That's wonderful.'

'The idea of shutting the café again for a week, just to write, makes me nervous,' Maya said. 'But it makes me excited too.'

'Excellent. Nervous excitement is the key. The nerves show you're going outside your comfort zone, and the excitement shows you're coming alive,' Sophie said. 'So, how about a month?'

Maya almost collapsed.

'Are you serious?'

Sophie shrugged. 'Why not be really bold?'

'Because I'm completely broke. I'm just about paying off my debts as it is.'

'Yes, and that'll be your life forever if you don't start taking some bold steps. I understand it'd be a stretch. But could you do it, without losing everything?'

Maya considered it carefully, then nodded nervously. 'Just about.'

Sophie said nothing. She just looked at Maya and smiled. In the silence she allowed the young woman to feel what was in her heart.

'It'd take a lot of courage,' Maya said finally, 'and a good deal of belief in myself.'

'Exactly, and your life isn't much of a life without that, is it?'

'No.' Maya sighed, briefly recalling so many monotonous moments in the café. 'It isn't. But what if I can't write? What if I waste the whole month?'

'A month following your heart is never a wasted month,' Sophie said. 'And, believe me, if you have the courage to do this, it'll set you on the path to your dreams.'

Maya closed her eyes and smiled, letting the words sink into her heart. But the fears and worries in her mind still clamoured loudly, not allowing her to be completely convinced.

Then she opened her eyes again to look at Sophie and something inside her started to fall quiet. Maya felt Sophie's peace and contentment slowly wash over her: a soft wave of self-love held her heart, a breath of compassion soothed her fears, and a rush of courage fired her spirit. She felt such a deep connection with Sophie that, for a swift second, it caused Maya to see clearly. In that moment she knew, in her heart and soul, that everything Sophie had said was true.

As Maya stood at the door she turned back to Sophie, suddenly remembering something.

'I forgot to ask,' Maya said. 'How do I listen to my heart?'

Sophie and Maya sat on the table, with a small pyramid of violet crystal between them, facing each other with their legs crossed.

'Is sitting *on* the table an important part of the process?' Maya asked, feeling utterly ridiculous.

'No, I just like it.' Sophie smiled. 'It offers a different perspective, don't you think?'

And there, sitting on top of the table, Sophie taught Maya how to listen to her heart.

*A*t first Maya was scared. So she'd decided to shut for only two weeks, despite a nagging feeling this was a betrayal of herself and her promise to Sophie. But she was far too nervous to do it for a whole month. Maya had considered hiring someone to run the café, but then she'd still have to keep tabs on things and that wouldn't be the same as closing properly. Sophie had specified a break, body, mind and soul. And Maya at least wanted to honour that.

For two days Maya sat in bed with Doughnut, wondering what on earth she was going to do next. She read books to distract herself, called Faith, watched a few films, ate copious amounts of damson truffles and chocolate flapjacks dipped in maple cinder toffee ice cream. She piled up these goodies and other snacks next to her bed, wanting to wander to the fridge as infrequently as possible, so she wouldn't notice her untouched computer sitting on the kitchen table.

At least five hundred times an hour it occurred to her to go downstairs and reopen the café, but Faith had promised to perform spontaneous checks to make sure Maya stayed the course. So she resisted and instead shifted onto the sofa.

Maya tried to convince herself she was just taking a little time to decompress, to relax and acclimatise to her new circumstances. She was in preparation, getting ready to write. But in truth Maya was terrified. She was terrified of sitting down at the computer and having absolutely nothing to say.

Halfway into the third day Maya got up. She threw her duvet off the sofa, tipping Doughnut onto the floor, took a shower, drank two cups of coffee, paced the kitchen for a while, fed Doughnut, tried to ignore a sublime slice of bitter citrus cake in the fridge, then finally sat down to write.

Two hours later the computer screen was still blank. And Maya had succumbed to the cake. The cursor blinked at her blithely. Maya stared back in despair. All her worst fears were being realised. She'd been crazy to believe in this plan. Who did she think she was? Having a dream to write didn't actually put words on the page. She couldn't do this. She felt like a failure and a fool.

Maya sighed and sank her head to the table. She sat like that for an age, unable to look up and face the blank screen again. Eventually Doughnut jumped onto the table and sat on her hair. Maya turned slightly to dislodge the cat without hurting either of them. A disgruntled Doughnut stood up and started licking Maya's nose. Despite herself, Maya smiled.

It was then she realised something. This was exactly what Rose and Sophie had talked about. It was exactly what they'd warned her not to do. She was swimming in thoughts. Fears, worries and doubts were overcoming her. And she was believing them, letting them dictate and create their own negative reality. Then Maya knew that she'd never achieve anything while listening to her head. It was time to talk to her heart.

Maya waited until dark, then crept downstairs to the café. She knew it was slightly strange to attempt this in the place where she often felt so miserable. But, on the other hand, the café was a place she felt safe.

When she was alone late at night she often thought of her mother, how she missed her, how much happier her life would be if Lily was still alive. Occasionally Maya would go down to the café and bake her mother's favourite cake: rosewater and white chocolate. Then she'd lean back against the counter, slide slowly to the floor, cross her legs and eat. Maya always made sure the cake was small, because the perfect taste combined with her sadness meant she'd eat every last crumb.

But tonight she didn't bake. She stood in the centre of the dark café and tried to get in touch with her heart. She conjured up the memory of her mother, without the assistance of tastes or smells, and felt the familiar ache in her chest. She spoke a few words, feeling silly, and half contemplated calling Faith, who'd surely be happy to help her with something so crazy. But, having come this far, Maya knew this was something had to do alone.

So Maya stood, a single figure in the empty space, eyes closed, feet apart, arms by her side, carefully remembering what Sophie had said.

'Stand in a solitary place and become quiet. Imagine your heart and consider it's more than just an organ. Instead it's the centre of your life force, and it beats in time with the pulse of creativity, of love. Imagine that it's your own guiding light; switch it on and it will brighten your path, leading you to the life of your dreams.'

'You can't be serious,' Maya had said, thinking Sophie must suddenly have lost hold of her senses. But the psychic had just looked at Maya with a knowing smile.

'We're all born with hearts that hold onto our dreams, keeping them safe from our negative and rational minds,' Sophie said softly. 'As children we follow our hearts all day long; we live according to our instincts and intuitions. But one day we stop listening to our hearts and start listening to the thoughts in our heads instead.'

Sophie sighed sadly. 'And when people stop focusing on their dreams they become lost in the maze of their minds, wandering around in endlessly repeating circles. Then the colours of life start to dull, and excitement starts to die. Until you're trapped in a prison of your own making, looking out at life instead of living it.'

Maya nodded slowly, knowing only too well how true this was. It described the progression of her life perfectly.

'Give it a try then,' Sophie urged. 'I know you think it's ridiculous and you'll feel like a fool at first. But whenever you're stuck in life your heart can give you answers. If you just dare to ask, I promise it will.'

In that moment Maya still hadn't really believed her, but thought now she'd give it a try. Because, why not? What did she have to lose?

So Maya stood in the café, feeling ridiculous. She imagined her heart as a guiding light and asked it to talk to her. She waited. And waited. But nothing happened. Then, just as Maya was about to give up, she realised she hadn't actually asked her heart anything.

'Okay, my heart,' Maya said out loud, feeling crazy and praying no one was watching her through the windows. 'I'm stuck and I need your help. I don't know what you can tell me. I guess I want to know if I should bother trying to write… I'm not sure that I can, it seems silly to even try. But there was that day in the library. I felt, for the first time in my life, I felt absolutely… sublime. Am I crazy to follow that feeling?'

After several minutes of silence, she heard it. Or rather she felt it, because her heart didn't speak with words, but feelings. Maya stood perfectly still as sensations bubbled up inside her. She listened as they gradually took the shape of her own voice.

'Should I write?' she asked again.

'*Yes. Start and don't stop. Soon your writing will be beautiful,*' the answer came. '*And through it you will experience joy.*'

'Can I make a living at it?'

'*One day,*' her heart said. '*But only if that is your intention. And you must follow that intention with many acts of courage.*'

Maya grew a little afraid at this and, as she started to sink into fear again, she almost lost the connection with her heart. Maya quickly centred herself.

'What about love?' she asked.

'*When you find compassion for yourself,*' her heart went on, '*you'll find love. Many men will want you, because there is nothing so attractive as someone who loves herself completely with a pure heart. So take your pick carefully.*'

'Is that all I need to find love? Compassion?' Maya asked.

'*Compassion, empathy and forgiveness are the cornerstones of unconditional love. But the first is the most important. Once you have that the other two will soon spring from it.*'

Maya waited, wondering whether or not to ask the question she now really wanted to know the answer to. Somehow she didn't feel she should, but then she didn't care.

'Is Jake the one?' Maya asked, but felt nothing. She strained to hear, but no answer came. Fearing the silence was itself an answer, she ignored it.

'Okay,' Maya sighed. 'Do you have any advice about how I could lose weight, once and for all?'

This time the answer came quickly, not through Maya's heart but through her body. Suddenly she was acutely aware of it, as though it was a living being quite separate from her spirit. She felt its aches and pains and its sorrows. She felt its longing to be cared for, to be loved and nurtured and accepted. She realised how it wept when she hated it, when she starved and deprived it, when she stuffed it, feeling how much it was despised.

'*As long as you hate me,*' her body said, '*I will be heavy, carrying the burden of that pain. Fill me with love instead of hate. For love is light and hate is heavy. Take care of me, nurture me, cherish me, love me absolutely. Begin exactly as I am, and I will put down the burden; I will let the weight go, and I will become as beautiful as I was born to be.*'

The next day Maya woke and started to write. Several hours later a story was taking shape and Maya could barely keep up with the words. Finally she took a break. Although she could have sat in front of the screen forever, Maya forced herself to get air. She walked to the park and sat in the sunshine for a while.

When she began again the experience was different. The words came slowly this time. And, ever so gently, they started to heal her. From heaven, from the ether, from the air, from everywhere, they floated into her consciousness. They hovered around until they travelled through her, to her fingertips and onto the keys. And, as they rushed through her body, they worked their magic, like tiny regenerative cells, links on little chains that brought all her broken pieces together and made her whole again.

Long after midnight, Maya fell into bed absolutely exhausted and completely happy. She realised she'd forgotten to eat all day. And, just as she closed her eyes, noticed she hadn't once thought about Jake either.

Maya had never dreamt work could be like this. Each day she set her alarm for eight but always woke just after six, excited and eager to write. And when she looked up at the clock again, hours and hours had passed in a second.

She gave herself until six o'clock every evening to finish. Sophie had suggested Maya spend her nights doing other things she loved, to nurture her spirit and soul. But it was hard for her to stop writing because it was so much fun. And when she noticed it was only three o'clock it filled her with joy that she had another three hours to keep creating.

In the café each hour had dragged by, a slow tick-tock of tortured boredom. She'd felt trapped in a hell of her own making. Now Maya was free. She'd stepped into a heaven of her own creation, feeling more alive than she'd ever felt in her life.

For Maya writing was an act of creating and an act of remembering. Odd and beautiful memories returned to her, gifts dropped into her lap, painting moments of joy and hope she had thought she'd lost forever. Maya's soul gradually took shape on the page and, for the first time in her life, she began to realise her own magnificence.

In her excitement Maya had stopped thinking about food and about Jake. Her mind didn't need to daydream because it was consumed with creativity. And her belly didn't bother her because she was full with words.

The two things that had weighed on her for so long had now lifted because of this one true step she had taken.

When the two weeks were up Maya knew she wasn't ready to open the café. She wasn't ready to let go of joy just yet. And this time she had no doubt in her mind.

Maya hurried downstairs to change the opening date on her sign, fear and excitement bubbling in her stomach. And, as she jumped down the steps, she noticed there was considerably less bounce in her belly. Maya ran across the café floor, reached the door, flipped the sign over, scribbled on it and then flipped it back. Then, just as she turned to go, Maya looked up and saw him through the glass.

Jake grinned and Maya gulped.

As he stood in front of her, and she contemplated whether or not to run away, she suddenly realised this was a moment she might never have the courage to seize again.

She was finally so happy, fulfilled and satisfied. She knew she didn't need a man, but she still wanted one. And her happiness had made her brave.

Of course, deep down in her heart, Maya knew it was too soon to get involved with Jake. She could still feel Sophie's words, about loving herself before loving a man, echoing in her head. And really she wasn't ready quite yet. But Maya was afraid the moment would pass and she'd never have the guts to grab it again.

As she opened the door Jake grinned, and she melted.

'Hi,' he said, walking in. 'I'm so glad you're back. I've literally been counting the days.'

Maya beamed happily.

'Yeah,' Jake said. 'If I don't get my morning caffeine fix I'm toast for the rest of the day. I can't stand all those bloody chains. The coffee is so bland. And they don't add chocolate cocoa beans to my cappuccinos.'

Maya's smile dropped. She followed him to the counter, feeling anxious. This wasn't going exactly as she'd imagined.

'Well, actually we're not really open…'

'Really? Not just for one desperate regular?' He flashed that smile again.

'Well, yes, I suppose… So, um, what would you like? The usual? I only have coffee anyway. I haven't had time to make cakes yet. But you never order them, so…'

'A cappuccino, please. A really big one.'

As Jake took his coffee and paid, Maya was seized by desperation. She couldn't let him go like this. She breathed deeply, summoning courage, remembering her mantra: *Don't live safe, live true.* So, she realised, asking Jake out wasn't about whether or not he'd say yes. It was about having the courage to express what was in her heart.

Of course Maya conveniently overlooked the fact that this desire didn't actually come from her heart.

She wanted Jake so much that it overrode all her instincts. If Maya had taken a moment to be quiet, to listen to the gentle whisperings of her heart, she'd have known this. But right now the clamourings of desire and desperation in her mind were too loud for her to hear a thing.

By the time Maya finally found her courage, Jake had reached the door.

'Wait!'

Jake turned back. Maya froze and waited for the earth to swallow her up.

'I, um,' Maya mumbled, 'I wondered if you might go… to dinner with me.'

Jake looked at her, surprised. The next ten seconds were the longest of her life.

'Sure,' he said finally. 'Why not?'

Maya sighed, able to breathe again. Enormous amounts of relief washed over her. It wasn't exactly the response she'd dreamt of. But it wasn't 'no'. And right now that was all that mattered.

$\mathcal{N}$ ow Maya had everything she had ever wanted. She was writing every day, dating Jake every night, and had lost almost a stone in three weeks. All she needed now was to make a little more money.

Most of all, Maya was in love. It was early days yet, and she had no intention of mentioning this to Jake, but she thought he really could be the one. She felt bad for judging him so harshly before, because now he was wonderful. And he seemed to like her too, which absolutely shocked and thrilled her. He wanted to be around her all the time and, whenever she wasn't writing or doing other things she loved, they met up.

Best of all, she didn't need to see him. She enjoyed it, but she didn't think about him when he wasn't there. She didn't count down the hours. She focused on whatever she was doing, gave herself to it completely, and was rather surprised whenever the phone rang. So it was always Jake who called and planned fantastic things for them to do.

And all their dates were perfect. They did fun and fabulous things: went to the ballet, the theatre, fancy restaurants, art galleries, walks in the park through the last of the autumn leaves. Jake organised all these things and paid for them. Which was lucky because Maya could barely afford a banana. He even bought her little presents, things she mentioned liking or wanting to try: opera music, jasmine tea, a red silk dress. And lots and lots of beautiful flowers, not a carnation among them.

This was what Maya loved most of all: that Jake really listened to her. He paid attention, he took mental notes, he responded only after really considering what she'd said. They didn't play conversational volleyball, with each waiting for their chance to speak; they absorbed each other, they had wild and wonderful talks.

The first night they made love brought Maya close to tears. A man hadn't touched her so tenderly in many years. In fact, since Rose, the only living thing to touch her had been Doughnut, who, despite being very cuddly, wasn't really much of a substitute for a loving relationship.

Jake was gentle and powerful. His kisses were hot on her skin and every time he came up for breath she arched her body towards his mouth again, pushing herself into him, still harder and faster, until finally they sank slowly down into a pool of pure happiness.

Maya lay in Jake's arms, unable to believe what had just happened. She glanced up at him and he kissed her.

'Are you okay?' Jake asked.

'No. I'm wonderful.'

In fact Maya was overjoyed. Not simply because she was in bed with Jake, but because she realised she didn't feel needy. She was so happy, so centred, so fulfilled, that she didn't need him. Life was glorious and Jake was simply a bonus.

'You're different from all the women I've been with,' Jake said. 'I love it.'

'*All* of them?' Maya smiled. 'You sound like a bit of a slut.'

'Shut up.' Jake laughed. 'I'm only saying I feel good when I'm with you, I don't feel like you're trying to trap me.'

'I'm not,' Maya said, and she meant it.

'I know, and I really love it. I love being with you. I don't want to lose you.'

'You're not going to lose me,' Maya said. 'Why would you think that?'

'I don't know. I just know I don't want to.'

Maya tipped her head up to kiss him.

'You're an incredible woman, Maya,' Jake said. 'You're so ... content. You accept me just the way I am. So many women want to change men, change them and trap them. But you don't. That's why I love you, you're so joyful in yourself that you just let me be me.'

'Well, I suppose that's because I don't need you to make my life beautiful, because it's already beautiful.' Maya smiled. 'I'm happy when you're here, and I'm still happy when you're not.'

Maya realised then that she really meant it. She wasn't just saying it to make Jake feel good. She was so pleased by this, so thrilled to finally love truly, without the twists and turns of need and dependency, that she almost didn't notice Jake had just said he loved her.

*M*aya adored every second of those blissful days away from the café and with her book. When she woke she waited for a few minutes, basking in the morning sun. Sometimes she meditated for a moment or two, before leaping up, ready to write.

When Maya settled down at her desk, coffee in hand, she felt more blessed than anyone in the world. She was allowing her heart its full expression, no longer squeezing it into the cracks of the day, but letting it fill every moment of her life.

When she wasn't writing she was taking long walks, bubble baths, meditations, dancing in her living room, sitting under trees and watching life go by: anything and everything picked for the pure purpose of nurturing her soul.

Finally Maya understood fully what Sophie had meant, about finding a life before finding a man.

This was the first time she'd really taken care of herself. The first time she'd made her happiness her number-one goal. And, just as Rose had promised, she spread her happiness to everyone she met, leaving little trails of contentment in her wake. Her smiles were infectious, her chatter uplifting and her laughter opened people's hearts so they felt that, whatever happened, everything would be okay.

When Maya wrote she could almost feel her soul spilling over with joy. This was her heart's desire and she was doing it. And, because she was too excited to eat, Maya could delight in the thrill of her new body. To top everything, she felt incredibly proud of herself for having the courage to take Sophie's advice.

*O*hen it was time to reopen the café. Maya had dreaded returning. She didn't want to let go of the happiness she'd finally found. She didn't want to betray her soul.

But Maya didn't know what else to do. In the last month she'd actually completed her novel, a rather autobiographical work of spiritual fiction, and thought maybe she could be bolder still and send it out to agents and publishers. This was a terrifying thought, especially because the book was so personal, and the process of writing it so magical, that the potential rejection was almost too painful to think about.

Maya's first morning back at the café felt strange, as though she didn't belong there any more. Maya still smiled while she baked, stirring the ingredients, sniffing the lavender sugar, pulling warm cherry-apple pies, strawberry crumbles, chocolate tarts and little apricot cakes out of the oven. But when she opened the café and sat at the counter she felt suddenly sad.

By the end of the day Maya was ready to cry. She'd had twenty customers all day. If she was going to survive financially she'd have to put a lot of energy into making her café a success. It'd take much more work. And she didn't want to put any energy into it. She just wanted to write.

That evening Maya seized the threads of her courage and set about posting her novel to publishers. She sat on the floor of her living room, manuscripts piled high, and began to fill envelopes. Doughnut weaved in and out of the papers as Maya worked.

'Hey, my sweet little fatty, stop that.' Maya picked the cat up and dropped her gently onto the sofa. Doughnut sat there for a moment before jumping back down onto a large pile of papers and spreading them everywhere.

All night Maya remembered what Sophie had said about positive belief and action being absolutely necessary to create the life of her dreams. So, while she stuffed the envelopes, Maya focused intently on the right people opening them, reading the first chapters, loving them and calling to ask for more. She imagined being published, inspiring other people to live their dreams, selling enough books to become a full-time writer, and living out the rest of her days feeling completely fulfilled.

It was a glorious night. Maya was so excited, so certain this was it, the beginning of an incredible journey, that she could almost feel the air around her buzzing. Several times Maya leapt up and did little victory dances around the living room. Every cell in her body tingled. It was the perfect culmination of her month of creativity. Doughnut smiled as she watched Maya manifesting her dreams.

Six weeks later Maya received her first rejection letter and it floored her. She simply hadn't expected it. She'd been so excited, so sure the first response would be a 'yes' that she didn't know what to think. Deep down her faith in Sophie, and her belief in the power of being bold, was dented a little. When, at the end of the month, every single one of her manuscripts had been returned with a rejection, her faith was completely destroyed.

Maya couldn't understand it. She'd done just what Sophie had suggested. But it hadn't worked.

That morning, in a fit of anger and despair, Maya closed the café, while the last rejection letter still sat on the counter. She wanted to smash everything near her, throw the cakes through the windows, and all the plates to the floor. Instead she slid down the counter and cried.

If Sophie had been there she would have told Maya not to give up. She would have reminded her that moments of greatest despair are when self-belief is needed most of all. She would have told Maya that this was just the beginning of her glorious journey, that she must pick herself up and keep going with belief and determination, because her dreams weren't so far away. But Sophie wasn't there and Maya didn't think to call her. Instead she called Jake.

That night Jake offered Maya distraction from her disappointment. He took her to the cinema and, as they sat in the back holding hands, kissing and sharing popcorn, Maya squashed her sadness and focused instead on being with him.

But, although she didn't realise it then, along with her sadness, Maya suppressed her belief in her dreams, because right now they only brought her pain. And so, in that moment, in a culmination of all the moments she'd ever given up on herself, Maya did it again. She thought that maybe she didn't need the writing after all; maybe just having Jake was enough.

'What?' Faith cried, after Maya had shared this thought with her. 'Have you forgotten what Sophie said? Are you forgetting to stay fulfilled?'

'I know, I know. I haven't. It's just that I can't write all day; I have to run the café,' Maya said. 'And, if I have to do that, I need some love in my life to see me through.'

'This is going to end in disaster,' Faith said. 'You want him to be the source of your happiness. It's not right. And you'll ruin the relationship. You'll become all needy and clingy and he'll run a mile.'

'Come on, that's not fair.'

'Hey, it's not fair of you to put that much pressure on someone. It's not his job to make you happy.'

'Stop being so spiritual,' Maya snapped. 'We can't all be like you, you know. We can't all exist solely on the source of universal love or whatever it is you call it.' Anger rose up in Maya's chest and she struggled with it, suppressing the urge to slam down the phone. 'Look, you may not understand it, but this is what real love is about, making each other happy.'

'No,' Faith said gently, 'that's not love. That's just not taking responsibility for your own life, for your own happiness.'

'Well, whatever you say. I'm not like you. I need a man to make me happy.'

'That's not true. Only a month ago you made yourself so happy that he was just a bonus in your life. You said so yourself. One of the many chocolate chips in your cookie,' Faith said, repeating the joke that had once made Maya laugh. But this time Maya was so wrapped up in a desperate need to be right, it only made her more angry.

'I've got to go,' Maya lied.

'Wait.'

Maya sighed.

'Sweetheart, I'm just trying to help,' Faith said softly. 'I know you want me to agree with you right now, to say you're doing the right thing. But I love you too much to do that. I'm telling you, if you want this relationship to work, you're setting yourself on the road to losing him. And it's okay if you hate me for saying it.'

Maya sighed again. 'I don't hate you. I just… I just don't think you're right.' But her voice no longer held quite as much conviction as before.

'Okay,' Faith conceded. 'Before you hang up, let me just tell you this. I've been going out with men lately, and it's been amazing. And I truly believe now that this whole idea of unavailable men is rubbish.'

'What?'

'I think most men want to be in love as much as we do. But sometimes women scare them off. We don't fulfil our own dreams and we expect them to do it for us. That's too much for any person to carry.'

'I don't…'

'Right now you're starting to sink back into a life that makes you miserable. And, instead of finding the courage to change it, you're thinking of investing your whole heart in Jake. And it's not fair. It's not fair on him and it's not fair on you. You both deserve better.'

A month later, although Maya now strongly suspected Faith was right, she'd still chosen to ignore her advice.

She tried not to think about the rejections, but the sense of disappointment and defeat left her unable to write. The monotonous days piled up one by one, weighing heavily on her heart. She didn't have the energy or inclination to do all the things she loved in the evening, and instead opted for the easier fix of seeing Jake.

And, very soon, these became the only moments of joy in her life. She'd got her man and now allowed all her other desires to fall by the wayside. And, although she couldn't shift a small sense of dread about what she was doing, Maya tried to forget what Faith had said and focused instead on being happy with Jake.

When Maya wasn't with him she waited until she would be. She watched the clock. She ate cookies to pass the time. She started to forget the solitary things that had once made her so happy. And after a while she just couldn't be bothered any more.

Maya started to call Jake, not just when she wanted to be with him, but when she didn't want to be alone. At first he came whenever she called, but then something started to shift between them. Jake began to withdraw a little and Maya started to need him more.

Maya knew what was happening; she could feel a pull towards Jake and wanted desperately to stop it. But, try as she might, she couldn't control her feelings. She had nothing else in her life. Only a café she hated being in, an overindulgence in chocolate, a growing unhappiness with her body, an emptiness in her soul. And Jake. He was the one source of pleasure in Maya's life and she was addicted.

The light of love was bright, so bright that it blinded Maya to the flicker of disharmony, the warning light flashing quietly inside her. And she ignored it two months later, when Jake stopped calling altogether and she started to feel her core unravelling in the wind.

Maya did everything she could think of to reclaim Jake and rekindle his feelings for her. Forgetting Faith, Rose and Sophie entirely, Maya now convinced herself that Jake was her one true source of fulfilment. And whenever her cousin called she just pretended everything was fine, then got off the phone as quickly as she could.

It was only when they slept together that Maya felt any sense of the intimacy she'd known in the beginning of their relationship. So Maya pestered him to make love, desperate to feel it again. On those nights she lay in bed as he slept, clinging to their dwindling sense of closeness, holding on tightly because she knew the feeling belonged only to the night and would be gone by morning.

Now, while Jake slept, Maya crept out of bed to read his phone messages in the dark, searching for clues of other women. But she never found anything incriminating, only new depths of self-loathing and despair she never imagined she'd reach. Afterwards Maya sat shivering on the edge of the bed, her heart racing, desperately wondering if she would ever feel okay again.

Maya never told Jake any of this, because she feared it would push him away for good. Instead she treasured every moment he came over when she called and grasped every hour they spent together. But, because she couldn't reveal her real feelings, Maya no longer shared herself at all. She kept everything inside, fearful of what might spill out if she spoke honestly about even the tiniest thing. So she just listened to Jake and only responded to whatever he talked about, nodding and smiling and agreeing with everything. Soon Jake was bored and Maya was hollow, no longer knowing what she thought or how she felt, no longer knowing herself.

Then their spark, tiny and barely flickering, went out.

But Maya wouldn't accept it. She tried to spice things up, tried to delve deeper into him, even though she knew his heart wasn't with her any more. At first Jake tried to be nice about it, but the more she pushed him the more he pulled away, until eventually he started being cruel.

When Jake told her he didn't think they should be together any more Maya was convinced he was wrong. So she stuck to him for another six months. No matter what he said or did, or how much it hurt. Until, finally, he left her.

That day Maya stood in the middle of the living room and screamed, while Jake sat on the sofa and Doughnut hid under it.

'I bet hundreds of men out there could love me!' Maya yelled, desperately wishing she believed it. 'Why does the one I love have to be such a total bastard? Why can't you love me? What the fuck is wrong with you?'

'I'm not a bastard,' Jake said softly. 'I never told you to give up on yourself, to give yourself away. I didn't ask you to. You did that without me.'

But Maya wouldn't listen, or try to understand.

'Why couldn't you love me?' she sobbed, feeling she was about to break in two. 'Why couldn't you just love me back?'

'I did. I did love you.'

Maya was about to yell again, but she stopped, open-mouthed, staring at him.

'But then you changed,' Jake went on. 'And you didn't love yourself any more.'

Still Maya couldn't speak.

'It's hard work loving someone who has given up on everything. And I can't… I just can't do it any more.'

Jake stood up and walked over to her. At first she pushed him away. Then he pulled her into a hug and held her tightly, just as Rose had done over a year ago.

'I'm sorry,' Jake whispered. 'I'm so very sorry.'

*N*ow Maya had nothing. Jake had gone; she hadn't written anything in over a year and was twenty pounds overweight. After Jake left she spent two days in bed, sobbing her heart out. Crying for everything she'd lost.

As she gripped her soaked pillow, sniffling, wiping her nose on her pyjama sleeve, Jake's words spun round and round in her head until she wanted to throw up.

Of course he was right. And Rose, Sophie and Faith had been right. And she'd ignored them all. Jake hadn't asked her to sell her soul to their relationship. She'd done that all by herself, because she'd been afraid of losing him. Because, when she gave up on her dreams, he was all she had left. But of course, even when she had him then, she'd still felt lonely and abandoned, like a poor orphan, desperately trying to convince someone to adopt her, instead of being a woman who knows her own worth: brilliant, magnificent, and confident she doesn't need to persuade a man to love her.

Maya sobbed as she remembered herself at the beginning of their relationship. She saw now what her fears had turned her into, and it broke her heart. Having completely abandoned herself, she was now overcome with the dark ache of feeling absolutely and utterly alone.

On the third day, with a great force of will, Maya made herself to return to the café. But, once there, she just sat behind the counter and cried. A few customers came by, and she served them through tears, but most people saw the sobbing woman through the window and just kept walking.

By the end of the week Maya had stopped crying and started eating. Day by day she worked her way through the leftover brownies, cakes and flapjacks on display, no longer caring about trying to stop. She couldn't face her pain; without chocolate she thought her heart might crack in two.

After work Maya continued to mourn the loss of Jake, wandering around the flat, lost in a haze of memories and tears. She missed the way he'd held her, listened and loved her. And, when she wasn't missing him, Maya was wishing she hadn't acted the way she had, pushing and pressuring him, until he'd no longer wanted her.

One night, a night of particular despair, as Maya soaked her sheets with tears, feeling more lonely than she'd ever felt before, she prayed for help. She prayed to God, angels, her heart, the cosmic forces, to anyone or anything that could possibly offer her comfort and relief from pain. Eventually exhausted from crying, Maya fell asleep. And, as soon as she did, she started to dream...

She was standing outside the café. The street was gone and had been replaced with an endless field of flowers. Hundreds of varieties jostled for space in the soil: white lilies, scarlet roses, soft-purple lisianthus, creamy-pink peonies and millions upon millions of daisies.

Maya smiled at the colours and the sweet,

intoxicating smell. She looked out to the horizon, until the ocean of flowers merged with the sunset. The sky mirrored the field, reflecting thousands of shades, so Maya felt she'd stepped into a sublime painting.

A woman appeared on the horizon, floating towards Maya. Then she touched the ground and walked through the field, gently parting the flowers, touching their petals with her fingertips.

For a moment, before she could quite make out her figure and face, Maya thought the woman was her mother and she cried out. An instant later she saw it wasn't Lily, it was Rose.

Maya smiled, a little disappointed but still happy. As they hugged, Maya nestled her face in the warmth of the old woman's neck, allowing herself to be held like a child. As Maya breathed, softly and deeply, never wanting to let go, a memory tickled the back of her mind, reminding her this must be a dream. For Rose was at least twelve inches shorter than Maya, so there was no way she could be holding her like this now. Maya pushed the thought away, quickly and easily, as she'd never been able to push away thoughts of Jake, and brought herself back to the comfort of Rose.

They held each other for a long time until suddenly they were separated, looking into each other's eyes. It was then Maya noticed they were floating above the field together.

'I have something to tell you,' Rose whispered. 'Something important.'

Maya looked at her and smiled. They drifted gently to the ground to sit among the flowers, soft cushions of peonies beneath them. Rose reached for Maya's hand.

'You're sadder than when I left you.'

Maya looked at the ground.

'I'm afraid I didn't take your advice,' she admitted softly. 'I loved a man before myself. And it all came to a rather sticky end.'

'I know, dear, I was watching.'

'Really?'

'I often tried to talk to you. But you weren't listening.'

'I know, I'm sorry. I wouldn't listen to anyone. Not you, not Faith, not my own heart.' Maya hung her head. 'I felt it sometimes, but I just wanted him so much, I didn't…'

'You were in the grip of fear,' Rose said gently. 'And for that I feel only great compassion for you.'

'Really? You don't think I'm a complete idiot? Ignoring your advice, obsessively holding on to him when I knew it was breaking my heart. Because I've been feeling horrible about me. I made a huge mistake. I was so, so stupid.'

Rose put a finger to her lips.

'Oh, sweetheart, please don't be so cruel to yourself. You didn't make a mistake. There are no mistakes, only life lessons you still need to learn.'

Around her, flower petals glowed in the fading sun, and Maya breathed a little more deeply, feeling some relief at Rose's words.

'But I still think I could have done it differently,' Maya said. 'I could have made it less painful. I was learning about love, true and false love, but…'

'And what did you learn?'

Having thought of little else over the past week, Maya knew exactly.

'False love is just wanting someone else, but true love is wanting someone else to be happy,' she said softly. 'I became so obsessed with Jake being my one source of joy, I wanted him so badly, that I stopped caring how he felt.' Maya laughed a little. 'It's insane, but at the end I almost felt like I could kill him for not loving me back. And I still thought I was loving him!'

At this Rose smiled so brightly she almost seemed to radiate light.

'Perfect. That is a great lesson.'

'But,' Maya protested, 'you warned me about this in the café. Why couldn't I have listened and learnt it then, without all this pain?'

'Oh, my sweet Maya,' Rose said, squeezing her hand. 'Don't be so hard on yourself. You did nothing wrong. Most people can't learn everything just from another person's advice. Of course we need it, because experience alone, without understanding, teaches us nothing. But people need to live their own lives too. Then they can use words of wisdom to shape their experiences and make sense of them.'

Maya listened. In the softness of the dream Rose's words dropped gently into the air, suspended, perfectly real and true.

'I understand now,' Maya said. 'About false and true love, about wanting and needing, about believing you desperately love the other person when you're really only thinking about yourself, driven by your own desires. I'll never do that again.'

'Well.' Rose smiled. 'You do understand a lot, but not everything.'

'Oh?'

'You need to know something else about relationships that will replace your pain with compassion. This will enable you to let Jake go and bring you back to yourself.'

Maya sat up, pressing her palms into the blanket of flowers, the promise of pain relief focusing her attention completely. 'What is it?'

Rose adjusted herself slightly, freeing a few flowers that sprung up from under her.

'Are you uncomfortable?' Maya asked, realising they'd been sitting for a while. 'Shall we move?'

'I can't be uncomfortable, dear,' Rose replied, smiling. 'This is a dream.'

'Oh, yes, of course.'

'But don't worry,' Rose said, reading her mind. 'Everything I say is still true.'

Maya smiled.

'So,' Rose continued, 'you need to know that relationships operate under emotional laws that are just as real and steadfast as physical laws like gravity. And when you're in a relationship you're subject to these laws, until you're enlightened.'

'Well,' Maya said, 'no chance of that just yet, so I guess I'm still a pawn to my emotions.'

'Wait a second –' Rose held up a finger. '– I detect a slight tone of self-judgmental harshness. We'll have none of that, please. Anyway, as you learnt when you started writing, enlightenment is much easier when you're alone than when you're with another person, especially a lover.'

Maya sighed. 'Why is that?'

'Our life lessons are magnified when we're in a relationship. It's like putting two people in a pressure cooker of needs, desires, fears, judgments and criticisms. Everything you do to yourself, everything you're trying to learn about and heal, you'll do to another person, and they to you.'

Maya nodded. 'Pain squared.'

'Exactly.' Rose laughed. 'Then they either help each other to heal, or they explode.'

Maya couldn't help but smile.

'So,' Rose continued, 'we each bring our particular lessons to the relationship and then, depending on how brave we are, how willing we are to learn, attempt to resolve and heal it with the other person.'

'Okay.' Maya considered this. 'So what are mine?'

'My dear, you have a few, we all do. But the main thing you and Jake struggled with was need.'

'Need?' Maya asked. 'Well, I know I began to need him too much, and that's what pushed him away. That's how I ruined the relationship.'

'Well,' Rose said, 'apart from the fact that you're being too harsh on yourself again, what you say is only partly true.'

'Oh?'

'This is why people get in such a muddle. They have a piece of the truth but they think it's everything. They think it explains why they're stuck in self-destructive patterns. But they don't realise that what they know is not the *whole* truth, because if it was it would set them free.'

'Oh,' Maya said, stunned. 'Please tell me the rest, please.' She could barely cope with the thought that she might have to go through another heart-breaking relationship experience again and still not learn the truth.

'Don't worry. I'm here to tell you. That's why I've come.'

'Of course.' Maya suddenly understood. 'You're here to save my life.'

'I'm here to offer you the wisdom to save your own life.' Rose smiled. 'You have to apply it in practice.'

'Oh, I will, I promise. Absolutely.'

'Okay then. Here is what I know.'

Rose separated her hands, holding them up as though she was balancing a ball of air in each palm.

'When we're born we need other people desperately, in order to survive. But, as we grow up, if our parents can't nurture us perfectly, if they hurt us, we desperately want to stop needing them, even though we still depend on them absolutely. Do you understand?'

Maya nodded. 'Just about.'

'This happens to most young people. Because even perfectly lovely parents can't hope to fulfil all of their children's needs. It's completely impossible. You'll understand this when you have children.'

'I'd have to stop repelling men first.' Maya smiled. 'So I'm not sure that will ever happen.'

'We'll see.' Rose laughed. 'Anyway, whatever the reasons, parents can then leave their children with one of two legacies: the fear of abandonment, or the fear of engulfment.'

'Eh?' Maya frowned.

'Well, you have the first one, because your father left you. And Jake has the second one, because his mother completely overwhelmed him and he just wanted to escape.'

Maya nodded. 'So we matched each other perfectly.'

'Yes, this is how relationships work. The life lesson is not to balance each other out, but to become balanced within yourself.'

Maya sighed. 'I wish I'd been able to do that.'

'Ah, but you didn't fail. The ending of a relationship doesn't mean failure. What if it couldn't succeed, if Jake simply wasn't the one for you? Then he just helped you see yourself more clearly. And the experience was perfect, just like you,' Rose said. 'Understanding the psychology behind romantic relationships isn't necessarily a formula to fix them all. It's a gift to heal our hearts and create long-term love with the right person. But some just aren't meant to last forever.'

Maya was listening so intently she hadn't noticed she was crying. However, she didn't feel pain, only a soft ache of sadness. As though she'd stepped into the emotion, like a gust of wind, to find it gentle and warm.

'It doesn't hurt,' Rose explained, watching her, 'because you're letting yourself experience it, you're not resisting it. Sadness is a sweet emotion if we let ourselves feel it. It reminds us we're fully alive. The pain only comes from resisting your sadness, from struggling not to feel it.'

Maya nodded, as every sweet puff of sadness blew through her body. Then it was gone. Maya laughed, suddenly filled with joy.

'That's the other thing,' Rose said. 'If you just let yourself feel it, then you'll come back to your natural state of peace and happiness.'

'Wow.' Maya said. 'That's wonderful.'

'That's life,' Rose smiled. 'Now, we have other things to cover. And I don't have long because you're about to wake up.'

'Please don't go yet. I need to understand the whole truth of what happened between Jake and me. Please. I can't… I really can't go through that again with someone else. I don't think I'd make it.'

'Don't worry, I won't leave without telling you, but we have to be quick.'

Maya nodded.

'When people live through their personalities,' Rose went on, 'they believe they need other people to make them happy. This is perfectly normal and actually quite fine and painless, except when we deny those feelings, which is when things get a little messy and painful.'

'How so?'

'Well, dear, like all couples who are uncomfortable with needing each other, you and Jake played a game. Imagine your need for each other was a hot potato you tossed around because you didn't want to hold it.' Rose lifted her tiny hands in the air again, as if balancing something carefully in each one.

'In a balanced relationship, you each hold fifty per cent of feeling you want and need each other. But, in the case of you and Jake, when you gave up on your writing and all the other things you loved, then the scales started to tip in your direction and you began to feel more and more of it.'

'And he began to feel less and less?'

'Exactly. So when you had seventy per cent of it, he only felt thirty. Until you held all of it, and he felt none of it. This is how a relationship can become completely unbalanced.'

Maya sighed. 'That's awful.'

'Oh, no.' Rose smiled. 'That is the key to your liberation. This need you felt, it wasn't all yours. You had his as well. You had your usual fifty per cent, and his too.'

'So I felt one hundred per cent needy?'

'Right.'

'But I'm not?'

'Of course you're not. When you were writing your book, you weren't needing people then, were you?'

'No. Not at all. I was completely happy by myself.'

'Well, there you go.'

'So when I was sobbing on the kitchen floor, feeling like I'd die if he left me, those feelings weren't real, they weren't true?'

Rose smiled. 'Now you're starting to see it.'

'That's incredible, I…'

'People play these games together; they just don't realise it,' Rose explained. 'One person, usually the woman, feels most or all of the need, so the other, usually the man, doesn't. Then, when the balance tips too far, she thinks she needs him completely and he believes he doesn't need her at all.'

'Why is it like that?'

'Well, of course it isn't always. But usually it's the way we're brought up. Distant fathers create girls who are used to feeling their neediness, so they take on that role in their relationship more readily. Overbearing mothers create boys who need distance in order to define themselves, so they more easily slip into the role of the partner who wants to run away.'

'Oh, I see.'

'Well, that's wonderful.' Rose smiled. 'Because once you really see that, once you know it deep down in your bones, then when it starts to happen again, you'll know it's not real and you'll stop it. Like a heroin injection you refuse to take.'

'It is like a drug then, isn't it?'

'And when you know this you're free,' Rose continued. 'The false feelings will just disappear. Then, instead of thinking you need a man, you'll be able to really love one.'

'That's fantastic.' Maya grinned. 'I wish you could whisper this to every woman in the world.'

'And the men too,' Rose said. 'I do my best, but they usually aren't listening.'

Maya opened her mouth to ask something else. But Rose put a finger to her lips and she stayed silent. They looked at each other, holding the gaze without glancing away. Gradually Maya sank into a deep level of understanding, seeing in Rose's eyes many of the truths she'd been searching for all her life. She was complete. She needed nothing. She had everything. She *was* everything: a perfect drop of God.

Then Rose vanished. And Maya was alone, staring out at the field of flowers. She wondered if she'd see Rose again. Suddenly she missed the old lady and her mother. That was when Maya realised. Rose was Lily. And Lily was Rose. And Rose and Lily were in everyone she'd ever met. Love wasn't just in one person, in one man. Love was everywhere. She'd just never seen it before, because she hadn't looked.

Maya opened her eyes, wide awake, staring up at the ceiling, letting it all sink in. Still basking in the vast splendour of universal love, Maya couldn't believe she'd been so fixed on Jake it had made her blind.

She hugged herself, laughing. The sound startled Doughnut, who jumped up, her ears twitching. Maya blew the cat a kiss.

'Hello, my gorgeously fat, furry friend!'

She threw the covers back, jumping out of bed and unbalancing Doughnut, who slid to the floor and looked up at her mournfully.

'Come on, grumpy.' Maya smiled.

Maya picked up the cat, walked into the living room and flopped onto the sofa. She squeezed and stroked Doughnut, who, magnanimously forgiving the earlier transgression, purred. Maya, feeling bright and born again, smiled and stared out into nothing. After a while Doughnut left Maya's lap, strolled across the carpet, jumped onto a desk hidden in the corner of the room and started meowing. Knocked out of her reverie, Maya glanced up to see the cat swishing her tail with purpose.

'What is it? What do you want?'

Doughnut kept meowing.

'Are you hungry?'

Maya pulled herself off the sofa and headed towards the kitchen, but halfway across the living room she stopped. She glanced back at Doughnut, who hadn't moved. Usually whenever she went to the kitchen the cat jumped up to follow. A strange shiver ran down Maya's spine. She walked over to the desk and picked up Doughnut.

'What is it?' Maya asked, stroking the purring cat.

She glanced down at the desk. Then, without knowing why, reached to open its drawer. There was her manuscript, untouched for a year. Maya sighed and smiled. Despite all the disappointment the book had brought her, the memories of writing it were still magical. Maya let Doughnut jump from her arms and picked up the book. She carried it over to the sofa. For a while she sat and stared at it, touching the cover and soaking it all in. Then she turned the first page.

Two hours later Maya turned the last page and closed her eyes. She blinked again to see Doughnut sitting next to her.

'You know what, gorgeous?' Maya asked, addressing the cat. 'After all those rejections I never wanted to look at that book again, but I actually rather liked it. In fact, I loved it.'

But the moment she spoke Maya was struck with a pang of doubt. Who was she to think it had any merit? She was the author after all, so was surely bound to like it. Thirty agents and publishers, all masters in their field, were unlikely to be wrong.

'Well.' Maya sighed. 'It doesn't really matter what I feel, because it's not going to change anything. If the rest of the world thinks my book is bad, that's all that counts.'

Maya's heart contracted. It hurt like hell to think that her dreams had all come to nothing, and resigning herself to it didn't make her feel any better.

Then a shaft of light cut through the darkness. Maya realised that in the last two hours she hadn't thought of Jake once. And she knew that, even if her creativity didn't matter much to the rest of the world, it still mattered to her.

When she went back to bed Maya couldn't sleep. But she wasn't thinking about Jake or chocolate; she was thinking about her book.

At about five o'clock in the morning Maya got up again and walked to the sofa where Doughnut was sitting on top of the manuscript.

'You know how important this is to me, don't you?' Maya asked, picking up the cat and reclaiming her book. 'Sometimes I think you care about me more than I care about myself.'

Maya returned to bed, slipped the manuscript under her pillow and slept soundly until morning.

The next evening Maya closed the café and caught a bus to Sophie's house. She hadn't called to make an appointment, or even to see if Sophie was home. Desperate to ask her something, Maya just prayed she would be.

As Maya approached her destination, she didn't know how to pluck up the courage to knock on the door, but knew she had to. She'd spent the last year giving up on herself; and it was time to stop. If she really wanted to live life, instead of merely surviving it, she couldn't give in to her fears any more.

Maya turned the corner onto Sophie's street and looked towards her house, expecting to see the purple sign. But the spot was empty. Maya stood on the pavement, dumbstruck and disappointed. She hadn't expected this.

Then she pulled herself together. Now was not the time to give into negative thoughts. Maya walked up to the door, drew a deep breath of courage and knocked.

After a while, as she was about to turn away, it opened. She turned to see a man standing in the doorway.

'Hi, um, sorry to bother you,' Maya said. 'I'm looking for Sophie.'

The man was about twenty years older than Maya, tall and handsome with kind, flirtatious eyes.

'You didn't bother me at all.'

'Oh, good,' Maya said. 'Is she here?'

'She left a year ago; she lives in Arizona now.'

Maya was so stunned she couldn't speak.

'I bought the house.' He smiled. 'She gave me a fantastic deal.'

'Oh.'

'Can I help you?'

'No, sorry, I'm fine. I'm fine.'

'Okay. Well then, have a lovely day.'

Maya glanced up at his green eyes. He reminded her, for a moment, of Rose.

'Thank you,' Maya said. 'You too.'

Maya went to sit on a bench across the street. She gazed at Sophie's house, overcome with disappointment, without a clue about what to do next. So she just sat, and waited until a better idea came along.

An hour later the front door opened and the man walked out. Maya looked up, thinking again how handsome he was. Then she remembered Jake. Happily, Maya noted, this now made her smile rather than cry.

Maya watched him walk across the road, until she realised he was coming towards her. Suddenly she was nervous, wondering if she should get up and leave before he reached her. But then it was too late. He stood in front of her.

'Hi,' he said. 'I'm Bill.'

'Hi,' Maya said, slightly anxious.

'I saw you out of the window. You looked a little lost. I came to see if you were okay.'

'Oh, I'm fine,' Maya said.

'Were you a client of Sophie's?'

'No, not really.'

'Well, maybe I can help you.'

'Why? Are you a psychic?'

'No, but I've been known to help people out from time to time.'

'Oh, I don't need any help,' Maya said.

Bill raised a quizzical eyebrow. Then Maya remembered how resistance never led to anything good, and how she'd almost missed out on the incredible experience of Rose and Sophie in the first place.

'Well, I suppose I do,' Maya admitted. 'And if you know anything about fixing broken lives, then I could certainly use the advice.'

Bill smiled and sat down. 'Go on.'

'Are you sure? Because I'm a little bit of a mess right now.'

'Oh, I think I can handle it.'

'All right then, if you say so.' Maya let a smile slip. 'Well, I've broken up with my boyfriend, although I feel okay about that now. I'm working in my café, paying off its debts, but I really want to be a writer. Oh, and I've put on at least twenty pounds in the last three months.'

'I see.'

'And I'm scared, because I don't know how to change it.'

'Hmm,' Bill mused.

'What?'

'It sounds like you've lost yourself trying to find happiness in external things.'

Maya sighed, as the truth of this sank in. Then she smiled. 'Are you sure you're not a psychic? You certainly sound a lot like Sophie.'

'Oh, yes?' Bill asked. 'What did she say?'

'She told me to believe in myself and be bold,' Maya said, 'and I was. I took a month off work and wrote a book. I tried to get it published, but I failed.'

'You failed?'

'To become a writer.'

'Really?' Bill asked. 'So, you're about to die?'

'What! No! Why would you say that?'

'You can't say you've failed to achieve something until you die,' Bill said. 'Or until you've tried absolutely everything; and you haven't really tried *everything* until you're dead. So you might have given up, but you certainly haven't failed.'

Maya couldn't help laughing at the seeming absurdity of his reasoning.

'So, since I'm not dead yet,' Maya smiled, 'what do you think I should do?'

Bill pondered this for a moment.

'Be bolder.'

'Sorry?'

'You should be bolder. When life doesn't work out the way you want it, it's not usually a sign you should give up; it's a sign you should be bolder.'

'Really?'

'Oh, absolutely. Not by trying the same things over and over again; but doing something radical, something brave, fresh and new.'

'Are you sure?' Maya asked, frowning. 'That seems a little crazy.'

'I know most people give up when life gets tough, but that's exactly when you need to give it everything you've got. If you feel like you've taken a fall, then it's time to take another leap.'

'But why?' Maya groaned. 'Why is it all so hard?'

'Well, I do have a theory about that.'

'Really?'

'I think we're all born with a purpose. Something we really want, a source of true joy.'

Maya nodded. 'It's writing for me.'

'Exactly. And that purpose, to write a work of inspiration, is the reward that motivates you through life. It encourages you to meet the challenges that will make you a magnificent inspiration to others. But that's why it's hard. Because if it was easy, then what would you have to teach others? What kind of inspiration would you be?'

'Ah,' Maya considered. 'Yes, I suppose so. And what might those challenges be?'

'Anything you need to do in order to fulfil your purpose.'

'Could you be a little more specific?' Maya asked, giving him what she hoped was a winning smile.

'Well, I usually find that these challenges, these soul lessons, are those things we find most difficult to do. The things we'd absolutely avoid if we possibly could.'

'Bloody hell, why's that?'

'I don't really know,' Bill admitted. 'But I've always imagined it's because we're meant to become fully rounded, complete beings. So, if we're avoiding something, then this is exactly what we need to face.'

'Oh,' Maya said. 'I see.'

'I think your main lesson is courage. I think you need to embrace being totally courageous. And when you've really done that, then you'll achieve your purpose.'

Maya sighed. It seemed that, no matter how hard she tried to avoid it, no matter how deep she buried her head in the sand, there was no escaping this particular challenge.

'And, when you take on and triumph over your challenges,' Bill continued, 'then you'll be rewarded with the life you long for.'

Maya nodded again. Although she didn't want to admit it, she knew this was true.

'You were brave to take a month off to write your book,' Bill said. 'I bet you were scared, but I bet you felt really fantastic too, right?'

'Better than I've ever felt in my life.'

'Wonderful.' Bill smiled. 'But if a publisher had simply accepted your book, that wouldn't have required any more courage from you, would it?'

'I suppose not,' Maya admitted.

'Then it looks like you haven't fully triumphed over that particular challenge just yet. You need to keep stepping into life until you couldn't be any more courageous,' Bill said. 'I think you'll discover that your joy comes from being the bravest, most glorious being you can be.'

'Really?' Maya grinned. 'And how do I do that?'

'Well, you could start with a little visualisation,' Bill suggested. 'Imagine being a truly magnificent woman, not a victim, not someone contained within boundaries and fears, but someone who seizes life and really lives it.'

'That sounds wonderful.' Maya smiled.

'And what would she do next?'

'I'm not sure.' Maya shrugged.

'How about publishing the book yourself?'

Maya laughed, until she realised Bill was serious.

'I can't do that.'

'Why not?'

'Well, I don't have the money for one thing. And, for another, the book obviously doesn't deserve to be published, or someone else would have done it.'

'Is that true?'

'Yes, of course. I think so. I suppose. I don't know.'

'Exactly.' Bill smiled. 'So, it's time to take another courageous step. To start becoming the magnificent woman you were put on this earth to be.'

'Do you really believe that?'

Maya looked at him incredulous, suspicious. Bill looked back at her, unblinking.

'Without a shadow of a doubt.'

*T*hat night Maya sat in the café, staring at her manuscript. She knew there was one thing she could do, if she really, really wanted to. It was, as Bill had said, only a matter of believing in herself and being bold.

Selling the café had never really occurred to Maya before. She'd certainly thought about quitting and hiring someone else to run it, but this could add several decades to paying off its debts. And she'd also felt tied to her mother's dream, and didn't want to disappoint her memory. But, most of all, she'd just never known what else to do. Without a degree the world wasn't exactly her oyster, and every time she'd thought about returning to university the fear of failure stopped her.

Now, as Maya contemplated what she might be about to do, she was seized by fear again. At least those other ideas had been sensible. Going back to university wasn't a guarantee of a fulfilled life, but it could probably promise a stable one. The idea of selling the debt-ridden café to publish her own book, a book that had been rejected by every publisher and agent she'd sent it to, absolutely terrified her. It was an insane proposition. If it failed she'd be left with nothing.

Eventually, exhausted by all this negative thinking, Maya fell asleep, her manuscript a pillow against the table.

Hours later she woke, blinking in the soft morning light. For a moment Maya forgot what she'd been thinking about the night before. Then her stomach sank. But, at the same time, she felt a buzz of excitement at the possibility of finally doing something truly courageous, something that would make her worthy of her own respect and admiration.

Then Maya grinned, suddenly forgetting her fear. She felt gloriously happy, ten feet tall and ready for anything. It was just as she'd felt over a year ago, when she'd shut the café to write her book.

Maya realised then that if this happiness was possible; if it only took courage to reawaken it, then she couldn't go back to misery, knowing she had a choice in the matter. That would simply be too tragic for words.

In the next few minutes, before she had time to wake up and let her rational thoughts take over, Maya rushed upstairs. On her kitchen table she crafted a quick *For Sale* sign, ran back downstairs and posted it on the café door. Then she got ready to open.

$\mathcal{A}$s she sat behind the counter, occasionally serving people coffee and cakes, Maya couldn't believe what she'd done. Her regulars reacted with shock at the news, sad to lose their favourite chocolate flapjacks and the cocoa beans in their cappuccinos.

Several times an hour Maya resisted the urge to run over to the door and rip the sign off. To distract herself, rather than eat, Maya delved into research about self-publishing. She sat at the counter with her laptop and investigated the various possibilities.

It certainly wasn't cheap, but she'd expected that. And while Maya had no idea how much she could sell the café for, especially since it was riddled with debt and clearly not the best investment in the world, she expected it would be just enough to cover the expenses. What on earth she would do after that, when she had no money and an enormous pile of unsold books, she had no idea.

But Maya remembered what Bill had said, about her challenges, about courage, about being a magnificent woman. And right now these things seemed more important than money or assurances or anything else.

As the day ticked by Maya noticed she wasn't just ignoring chocolate because of her slight fear-induced nausea, she actually wasn't interested.

It was then, staring at the vanilla-strawberry biscuits, chocolate macaroons and coffee eclairs, Maya realised they didn't have any hold over her and never had.

Her overwhelming desire for them hadn't been about their gooey insides, their moist softness or their creamy toppings. It was really about her desire for a better life: a life so magnificent she could barely breathe. This is what Maya wanted whenever she reached for a slice of cake: a tiny taste of happiness.

But of course the fleeting pleasure of food was a poor substitute for the deep, forever pleasure of living a brilliant life. And the same went for romance and money. As part of a truly glorious life they might be lovely, but as substitutes for it they simply didn't work.

Now Maya saw that whenever she lived that life, when she wrote her book, when she decided to sell the café, she couldn't care less for cookies. Suddenly they faded into the background and became part of life's decoration, just like everything else. The idea that she used to spend all day thinking about them, trying to resist them, seemed crazy to her now. Maya sat at the counter and smiled at how much power she'd once given these illusory desires over her true dreams.

As six o'clock approached Maya had found the right company to publish her book. She switched off her laptop with a smile and walked to the door to close the shop. As she flipped the sign over she glanced out of the window to see Tim passing by. Maya waved, but he couldn't see her, so she opened the door.

'Hey.'

Tim looked up, grinning as he saw her. Maya drew a breath. She hadn't seen him in more than a year and had forgotten how beautiful he was. Or maybe, in her exclusive focus on Jake, she'd just never noticed before.

'You're here. You're alive.' Tim exclaimed. 'How are you? Where have you been?'

'I've... I... I...' Maya stumbled, not wanting to explain. 'I went on a video diet.'

'I missed you, and your cakes.' Tim smiled.

Maya felt suddenly overcome with the desire to kiss him. After months trying to persuade Jake to want her, it was a relief to be with someone who clearly did.

'I missed you too.'

Then Tim noticed the sign.

'You're selling The Cocoa Café? I don't believe it. Why?'

She shrugged, too embarrassed to tell him her crazy plan. 'I, um, I suppose it just feels like the right time.'

'How much are you asking?'

Maya shrugged again, unable to concentrate on finances when Tim now seemed so kissable.

'I don't really know. Not much. I think I'll just see what people offer.'

'Be careful you don't get fleeced.'

'Oh, it's not worth much. It's just the name and reputation. It still has debts…'

'Does the sale include the flat?'

'No, I rent it. Why?'

'Oh,' Tim considered. 'Okay then, how does a hundred grand sound? I can give you ten now, and the rest in six months. How about it?'

'Are you teasing me?'

'Of course not,' Tim said. 'I'm serious. This place would be great for another video shop. Business was excellent last year, so now we're expanding.'

'You're expanding?' Maya was confused. 'I thought you just worked there.'

'No, I own it. Well, we own it.' Tim held up his hand to reveal a wedding ring. 'My wife's invested in it too.'

Maya gripped the doorframe for support.

'W-wife?' Maya stuttered. 'You're married?'

'Yep, three months now.'

'Oh, I, wow, that's… wonderful. So, um, how did you meet?'

'She was a customer.' Tim smiled. 'She just kept coming in, and we started talking. And then we fell in love.'

'Well, that's, that is… wonderful,' Maya said again, wanting to crawl into a hole and cry.

'Vicky is lovely.' Tim grinned. 'And she likes sci-fi films. Which is pretty much the foundation to our love. I could never convince you of the charms of *Star Wars*, could I?'

Maya shook her head, trying to smile.

'Anyway, what do you think of my offer?'

Maya couldn't think about anything, so she just nodded. She only wanted to take the money and run. She had to get out, out of the café, out of the town, out of the country.

Maya had a sudden urge to follow Sophie to Arizona, to make a fresh start, to be a magnificent woman with no memories.

'Yes, it's… it's a great offer,' Maya managed to say, 'but since I'm still about eighty grand in debt, it's not really…'

'Ah,' Tim considered, 'well then, if I take on the debts, that leaves you with twenty thousand. How about that?'

Maya nodded slowly, unable to take it all in.

It was all happening so fast. She'd imagined it would take months before someone made an offer, and even longer before she actually got her hands on any money, giving her plenty of time to back out at the last minute.

But here she was, about to make a verbal agreement. It looked as though she wasn't going to be allowed to mess around with this decision after all.

After they'd agreed on terms and Tim had left, carrying a box of coffee eclairs, jasmine macaroons and chocolate flapjacks, Maya sat down. She couldn't believe what she'd just done, and she couldn't believe Tim was married.

It was a dreadful realisation, because here was her addiction to unavailable men raising its ugly head again. First Jake, now Tim, who she certainly hadn't wanted until he no longer wanted her. Maya wondered what exactly was wrong with her.

Then, suddenly remembering her realisation about chocolate, Maya knew nothing was wrong. She'd been scared to sell the shop and publish her book and, for a moment or two, had distracted herself from the fear with the promise of romance.

Maya breathed a sigh of relief. If she'd jumped into a relationship with Tim she would have turned it into the same relationship she'd had with Jake.

She'd have used him, as she'd used cakes, to avoid doing the brilliantly scary thing of fulfilling her true heart's desire. Just as she'd stopped writing and started living through Jake, she would have stopped self-publishing and started living through Tim. Because, painful as losing herself in a relationship was, it obviously seemed safer than going out into the world and taking terrific risks in the pursuit of her dreams.

Maya laughed then, as she saw her addiction for what it was. She'd tried to use men as safety blankets. Instead of finding a soulmate – someone who would encourage her spirit to soar, who'd partner her in a magnificent life – she'd used them as unwitting suppressors, substitutes for living courageously.

But a man wasn't a substitute for a life. He wasn't a pit stop you stayed in too long because you were too scared to fully express yourself. Now Maya understood. She knew that, if she was to find a soulmate to join her journey, she needed to begin it alone.

A month later Maya stood in the empty café. Everything was gone: the counter, the coffee machine, the tables, chairs and all the cakes.

Maya thought of her mother and felt a soft wave of sadness come over her. She knew Lily had always wanted her to be happy. Keeping the café hadn't really been due to Lily's legacy but because of her own fears. Then Maya smiled, realising that, in selling the café, the weight of a lifetime of fear had lifted and she was finally free.

Upstairs the flat was also empty. She'd sold everything and all that remained were a thousand copies of her book. When the printers asked her how many she'd wanted Maya had settled on this number. It had sprung up in her heart and, although it seemed completely insane, it also felt right. Bill had told her to be bolder so here she was being bolder. And it felt wonderful.

Maya locked the café doors for the last time, blew her mother a goodbye kiss and crossed the street without looking back. As she walked away, Maya understood that, although she'd spent so many years feeling trapped, The Cocoa Café had ultimately been a gift, now giving her a new direction in life. However, before she left England, she still had one more thing to do.

Faith opened the door and stared at Maya, unable hide her shock. Then she smiled, pulled her cousin into a hug and invited her in.

Moments later Maya sat awkwardly on the sofa, not knowing what to say. She hadn't spoken to Faith in over six months and couldn't begin to think how to make it up to her. A thousand thoughts raced through Maya's mind, falling on top of each other and collapsing in a heap.

'I'm so, so… really so sorry,' she whispered at last, holding back tears.

'It's okay,' Faith said. 'I know what happened.'

'You do?'

'Jake.'

Maya nodded.

'But it wasn't really his fault,' Maya said. 'I did exactly what you told me not to. I gave up on myself and I made him my whole life. And he ran a mile.'

'When you stopped calling, I guessed…'

'I really am so sorry.'

'Don't be, honey pie, I understand.'

Maya smiled gratefully. One of the things she loved so much about Faith was how forgiving and accepting she was. She didn't get self-centred about life; she didn't demand that people change themselves to fit her needs and desires. She just let them be. And it made them, and her, so very happy and relaxed about life.

'Thank you,' Maya said, considering what a wonderful lesson in enlightenment her cousin was. 'Thank you.'

'So, how are you now?'

'Pretty good, actually.'

'That's fantastic,' Faith said, genuinely happy, not holding a grudge for a second.

'I'm going to America.'

'Really?' Faith asked, wide-eyed. 'That's wonderful. For a holiday, a visit…?'

'I'm going out there to sell my book.'

'Your book?'

'Yep, I published it myself. I sold the café, I printed a thousand copies and now I'm going to try and sell them in America. I know it's crazy, but I think it's about time I did something wild with my life.'

'It's not crazy,' Faith said. 'It's fantastic!'

Maya smiled. 'I knew you'd understand.'

'Shall I look after Doughnut while you're gone?'

'That'd be lovely. Only…'

'What?'

'I have this strange feeling.'

'Yes?'

'That I might not be coming back.'

'Really?' Faith grinned. 'I didn't know you had intuitions like that.'

'I don't. I don't know why I feel it, I just do.'

'Maybe it's because you're finally really living your life,' Faith said. 'You've stepped into line with the universal vibes and can now attune fully to the cosmic forces.'

'That's one of the many, many things I love about you, Faith.' Maya laughed. 'You're not afraid to be a little nuts.'

Faith laughed too, not at all offended.

'Actually, I'm slightly nutty myself nowadays,' Maya admitted. 'And happier than I've ever been in my life.'

'Yes, well, I've found the more you live true to yourself, the happier you are,' Faith said. 'And the nuttier other people think you are.'

Maya was suddenly overcome with love for her cousin, who accepted her so unconditionally. She shifted across the sofa and pulled her into a hug.

When they finally separated Faith kissed her on the
cheek.

'I'm really proud of you, May.'

'Yeah.' Maya smiled. 'I'm proud of me too.'

*M*aya snuggled down in her airplane seat. A hundred books were in the cargo hold, the rest were following her on a ship, and she had only a few thousand pounds left in the bank. Maya grinned. This was far and away the craziest thing she'd ever done, and she was loving every minute of it.

Maya glanced at the old man sitting next to her. He'd caught her attention several times over the last few hours and she was curious to talk to him. And, since she was now a woman of courage, she realised this shouldn't be much of a problem.

'So –' Maya turned to him cheerily '– do you live in New York? Or are you going on holiday?'

The old man looked at her.

'Well, well,' he said. 'How nice to have a pretty young woman strike up a conversation with an old codger like me.'

Maya smiled.

'I'm Thomas.'

'Maya.'

'Really?' he asked, thoughtfully. 'Do you know what your name means?'

Maya shook her head.

'To the Hindus the veil of Maya is what covers our eyes when we see the world through our minds: with all our judgments, criticisms, fears and doubts. But the world beyond the veil of Maya is the world you feel through your heart. When the veil falls from our eyes we experience enlightenment. But until then we are blind.'

Maya's eyes widened. This explained a lot.

'I can't believe I never knew that,' she said. 'But it doesn't really surprise me. I've spent most of my life being blind.'

Thomas patted her hand affectionately. 'So have most of us, dear, so have most of us.'

'But not any more,' Maya said proudly. 'Not now.'

'Oh yes?'

'I'm going to New York to sell my book.'

This was the first time she'd said this to a stranger, and with such confidence she felt like a different person. Perhaps she wasn't Maya any more, at least not the Maya she'd always known.

'Well, well, that sounds fantastic. Was it a big hit in England?'

'No,' Maya admitted, 'I didn't sell it there. I've published it myself. But it's sort of a spiritual book, about my journey from cynicism and bitterness to self-belief and happiness. And I think the Brits aren't quite as receptive to that stuff as the Americans. So I thought I'd start over here.'

'Well, that's very brave of you. I'm extremely impressed.'

'Thank you.' Maya grinned, thrilled. Feeling courageous made a wonderful change from feeling like a pathetic mess. 'I'd have never done it alone though. I got a lot of help, and a lot of encouragement.'

'That's okay,' Thomas said. 'I don't think any of us can do it alone. I don't think we're meant to.'

'I even saw a psychic once,' Maya admitted.

'Oh, I've done much crazier things in my long life, I promise you.'

'Really?' Maya was intrigued. 'Well, actually my psychic was wonderful. She didn't really predict my future but told me about my own spirit, about how to follow my path in life. She told me to be bold.'

'Ah-ha. Well, that's very good advice.'

'Yes, it was. Very difficult, but very good. And I was just about to give up on the whole thing when I met this chap, Bill, who told me to be even bolder.'

'Ah, I see,' Thomas said. 'Isn't it amazing how wonderfully well life works when we follow our feelings, when we listen to our hearts instead of our heads?'

'I'm not sure,' Maya said. 'I think I just got lucky. I wasn't really following my feelings. I was pretty stuck and scared.'

'Maybe. Or maybe you only thought you were.'

Maya considered this.

'What's the difference?'

'Your thoughts about yourself, your life, about anything actually, they aren't always real. They don't always relate to actual facts. Indeed, they often don't.'

'Really?' Maya asked, intrigued.

'Oh, absolutely,' Thomas smiled. 'You can have the thought *I'm bored*, for example. Or *I'm stuck*, *I don't know what to do next*, *I'm scared*. And you're not. But you hear it in your head, so of course you believe it. And then you act on it, and it becomes real for you. That's what makes it true, even though it's not.'

Maya looked at him, and for a moment everything seemed to stand still. This had never occurred to Maya before. She had always believed her thoughts about herself were true. But maybe they weren't.

Maybe these thoughts were nothing more than just… thoughts.

'So, how do I know if I'm having a real thought or not?'

'Real thoughts are completely neutral, without any judgment,' Thomas explained. 'They acknowledge something, and then they pass. But if they create emotions in you, especially fear and pain, you can guarantee they aren't real.'

'So, if they aren't real, where are they coming from?' Maya asked.

'Oh, anywhere and everywhere. It doesn't really matter. The mind is a sponge. Anything you've ever heard and continue to recycle over and over again. A hundred million beliefs, judgments, criticisms, ideas, all spinning in circles – a crazy radio that one day, if you're very lucky, you will switch off and set yourself free.'

'And then I'll stop thinking altogether?'

Thomas smiled. 'Only in very rare cases. Maybe if you spend the rest of your life on top of a mountain.

For the rest of us the thoughts never cease, but we can stop listening. We can stop believing them. That's the secret.'

'That's wonderful,' Maya smiled. 'Absolutely wonderful.'

Now, in the bright light of this new knowledge, Maya saw that she hadn't been a stuck, scared mess; she had only thought she was. It was just those fearful, critical thoughts that had kept her tied to her life, nothing else. It was then Maya realised that there really was nothing wrong with her at all.

'So,' Thomas said, 'if you ever believe you're stuck again, just ignore those thoughts; become aware of your feelings and follow them instead. That always works for me.'

Maya grinned. It seemed that, when she opened up enough to actually connect with people, most she met had something helpful to say. And she knew that, with eight billion people in the world, this help was available to her all the time. She just had to be brave enough to ask. Then Maya realised that, of all the strangers who had approached her with advice along the way, meeting Thomas was the first time she'd made the first move.

'Thank you. Thank you so much,' she said, squeezing the old man's hand and giving him a little kiss on the cheek for good measure.

It was in the next moment that everything Rose had said finally fell into place. Wisdom met experience, and the third cornerstone to Maya's amazing life was laid down. Compassion. Courage. And connection.

Maya beamed as they landed in New York. She helped Thomas off the plane, found their luggage, grinned at the customs officials and then caught a bus into Manhattan.

As the skyline came into view it was all Maya could do not to clap her hands and whoop with joy. She pressed her nose against the window, staring out of it unblinking, until the bus swung into the Lincoln tunnel. When she stepped out of the station and saw her first yellow taxicab Maya could contain herself no longer. She dropped her suitcases and jumped up and down with joy.

That night, as an act of faith and celebration, Maya stayed in a fancy hotel and ordered room service. And as she snuggled down into silk sheets she breathed a deeply satisfied sigh, closed her eyes, and tingled with the special thrill that only comes from following your dreams.

A week later Maya wasn't having much luck. None of the big bookshops would take her book because they only did deals with proper publishers. Maya felt rather dejected about all this and slightly sorry for herself. After the third day and the thirteenth rejection, she started thinking the world was at fault, that it was a tough, hard and unforgiving place.

Unfortunately she'd forgotten for the moment what Thomas had said about not believing *all* her thoughts. If she had remembered that, and was honest about the quality of her efforts, Maya would have acknowledged she wasn't really keeping her end of the bargain. All alone in the big city, and a little overwhelmed with fear, she took the rejections a little too readily and didn't really do all she could do to promote herself with gusto.

Two weeks later Maya had exhausted the last bookshop she could find in Manhattan and didn't know what to do next. Of the thirty-three bookshops she'd been to only four had accepted any of her books. With such a poor success ratio Maya couldn't really face begging her way around Brooklyn or the other boroughs. In truth she was quite ready to give up, pack up and go home.

But, after all she'd been through, Maya couldn't go back; she had to keep going forward. Following Thomas's advice, she stood in the doorway of a shut-down shop on Amsterdam Avenue and tried to tune out of her thoughts and into her feelings, to see what her next move should be. But after a while she hadn't received any particularly strong messages. Her heart was rather quiet, only suggesting she let go a little and give up trying to sell any more books that day.

So Maya headed downtown, walking wherever her inclination took her, and ended up in the West Village, standing next to a beautiful pavement café in a lovely street full of pretty, unique shops.

Maya sat outside and ordered a coffee and chocolate croissant, for old time's sake. An hour later, the croissant still untouched, Maya watched the sun go down. As she absorbed the sights and sounds of the street, she began to relax completely, all her recent disappointments fading with the soft light.

Maya glanced up as the last, long rays of sun shone through the trees, and a song popped into her head: '*If you're going to San Francisco, be sure to wear some flowers in your hair…*'

Maya sat up straight. She wasn't sure if it was the light, or the coffee, or because she'd always loved that song, but right then Maya felt she'd just been given a sign.

San Francisco would be perfect. It was, after all, the spiritual Mecca of America. Everyone knew that the esoteric types migrated out there, whereas New Yorkers were supposed to be a little more cynical. And, since she'd left England because she didn't think her book would survive the cynicism, there wasn't much point in staying here.

The next day Maya and her books boarded a bus heading west. In seventy-two hours she would be there.

When Maya stepped off the bus three days later she wasn't feeling quite so sure of herself. She'd swapped New York for another city where she knew no one and had no clue how to best execute her game plan. After so many hours on a bus, with pit stops at all hours of the day and night, Maya was so tired she just wanted to crawl into a bed and cry.

The next day, feeling reinvigorated and refreshed, Maya packed ten books and a city map, and set off to conquer San Francisco. From various midnight chats with fellow passengers Maya had gleaned a little information about where to start. And in the cool, clear light of morning some of it was beginning to come back to her.

She boarded a streetcar and headed downtown, which, according to her sources, was supposedly a haven of receptive, friendly people eager to help anyone a little lost in their lives.

The streetcar was enormous fun, and the speed and scenery made Maya smile again. She would have happily ridden it all day, in a magnificent loop-tour of this glorious city she was already starting to love. But Maya knew she had a job to do, lessons to learn and a purpose to fulfil. And now wasn't the time to chicken out. So she hopped off the streetcar and stepped into the crowds of people pushing their way down Haight Street.

After an hour, and two cups of herbal tea, Maya felt it was time to venture off the main street, which seemed more of a tourist attraction than the heart and soul of the city, and into the little side streets in search of a bookshop to accept her book.

Maya was beginning to get used to following her feelings, using her heart instead of her head to direct her, and noticed the more she did the easier life became. She suffered fewer setbacks, experienced more synchronicities and happy coincidences, as though she was floating down a stream instead of fighting against it.

Having now travelled across America, albeit rather rapidly, Maya was developing a sense for places and noticing how each area had its own particular vibe.

Driving across Arizona at dawn, she'd been overcome by the vastness, the stillness of the mountains and the serenity of the silence they sat in. Having spent her whole life in a small English town, Maya had never seen such huge cliffs up close. As the sun came up she'd gasped at the magnificence that surrounded her. This was a place she vowed to return to.

San Francisco was also beautiful: open, accepting, curious and kind. Maya could feel these sensations in the air and hoped the same qualities were in the people.

After a little while Maya stopped walking. She'd wandered far off her initial path and now stood in front of a tiny store declaring itself to be The Alternative Bookshop. Taking a deep breath, Maya pushed the door open and walked in.

A bell tinkled above her, instantly transporting Maya back to the café. As she stepped inside she smiled. The shop was lined floor to ceiling with new and second-hand books. The floors were wood and the ceilings painted with deep blue skies and gold stars. Maya wandered slowly alongside the shelves, tracing her finger along the oak, following the maze of book-laden paths to a counter tucked away in the back.

A man sat behind the desk, engrossed in a book. Maya watched him for a few minutes, thinking that perhaps this wasn't the best place to try and sell her books after all. Then, as she was about to turn and go, he glanced up. Maya held her breath. Here was just about the loveliest man she'd ever seen.

He wasn't over-the-top gorgeous, with high cheekbones and a chiselled chin, but he did have big, deep brown eyes that a woman could get lost in if she wasn't careful. He looked at her and, for a moment or two, Maya lost all track of what she was thinking and why she was there.

'Can I help you?'

'What?' Maya came to her senses. 'Sorry, I, um, yes, I'm here to see you about…'

Maya pulled herself together to focus on the matter at hand and not the man. No doubt he was married, gay or unavailable in some other way, if past experience was anything to go by. And, since she needed every ounce of courage to go the distance and fulfil her dreams, she couldn't afford to get distracted by romance right now.

'I wanted to ask if you'd accept some of my books for sale? I could leave you a copy, if you want to think about it.'

The man studied Maya, seeming to consider her proposal. Then, to her delight, he nodded.

'Sure,' he said, 'let's have a look.'

Maya opened her bag, pulled out a copy before he could change his mind, and handed it over, nervous but proud. He examined the cover, reading aloud.

'*Men, Money and Chocolate*, by Maya Fitzgerald.'

Maya nodded and smiled hopefully.

'Intriguing title. What's it about?'

Maya breathed deeply. This was the embarrassing part, the moment she dreaded most.

'Well,' she began in one breath, 'it's… it's sort of autobiographical. About my journey from being lost in a world of thoughts and desires… my obsession with men, money and chocolate, to eventually finding my heart and soul… and discovering that true happiness doesn't come from those things, but from following your dreams and becoming the… the most magnificent being you can be.'

Maya managed a quick smile before she started to cough. Then she couldn't stop. She gripped the counter and bent over, her head between her knees. She felt the man watching her and wished she could disappear in a puff of smoke.

'Sounds great,' he said finally. 'I'll take ten copies.'

After a moment Maya managed to stand, smile and resist the urge to hug him. 'Really? That's incredible, thank you. Thank you.'

'Absolutely. Although I'm afraid I can't pay you now, only if they actually sell.'

Maya deflated a little. 'Oh, of course,' she said, pretending this wasn't a surprise.

'Fantastic,' he said. 'So, Maya Fitzgerald, if you just give me your number, I'll call you as and when we sell them.'

Maya, who was quickly emptying her bag of books, nodded and looked for a piece of paper on which to scribble the number of her B & B.

'I'm only here for a week,' Maya explained as she wrote. 'I'm doing a little tour of America, trying to sell books as I go…'

'Really? Wow. Where are you going next?'

'I'm not sure.' Maya shrugged. 'I haven't planned it all out. I'm going to see –'

'– where the wind takes you.'

Maya smiled. 'Yes, I suppose so.'

He stood and reached out his hand.

'Well, nice to be doing business with you, Maya. Here's my number so, after you leave, you can call me to check on the progress of your book.'

Maya took his card and glanced at it:

Ben Matthews, <u>The</u> Alternative Bookshop: 415 948 8490, specialising in books that will open your heart and blow your mind.

Maya shook his hand.

'That's wonderful, Ben. Thank you.'

The following day, buoyed by her success, Maya took a tour of the city. She wasn't interested in the big tourist sites; she wanted to get the real feel of the place, to explore the nooks and crannies, the hidden secrets that made it special.

Maya meandered along the streets, stopping off in shops and cafés, chatting with strangers and smiling at their stories. Finally she came to a park where all the crowds fell away.

Maya realised then that she'd spent the whole day being with people, random souls for brief moments, and she'd loved every minute of it. Most of all she enjoyed who she was now. It no longer took courage for her to connect. She was beginning to live her life fully, without holding back or second-guessing herself every step of the way.

Maya crossed a wooden bridge to an island in the middle of a lake. Looking out across the water, Maya noticed she felt as peaceful as her surroundings, silent in her mind and still in her heart. It was then she knew that it didn't really matter whether or not she sold her books, or whether anyone read them at all. Of course she'd like that, as another form of connection, but Maya was no longer desperate for it; she didn't need it to make her feel successful.

Maya wandered along a path and through a cluster of trees until she reached a waterfall. She found a big, shiny black rock and sat down. Icy cold water splashed into a stream that rushed beneath her feet. She slipped off her shoes, dipped her toes in, and laughed.

As the sun began to sink behind the trees Maya stood, picked up her shoes and walked barefoot into a clearing to catch the last rays of light. Across the lake the red tip of a giant pagoda peeked out of a little forest, marking the entrance to the Japanese Tea Garden.

Maya was delighted, having always wanted to see it. She strolled towards the garden, through the woods, gazing at the setting sun. But when she reached the gates they were closed. For a second

Maya was disappointed, then she just smiled and promised herself she'd return tomorrow.

The next morning Maya woke early. She took the streetcar across town, then headed towards the garden, visiting a few little bookshops along the way. To Maya's delight each one took five copies of her book. Everyone was so positive, lovely and welcoming compared to the New Yorkers, and Maya wondered why.

It was then she realised the next big lesson in her life. Those people hadn't been unfriendly because they intrinsically were; they'd been unfriendly because she hadn't really opened up to them. She'd expected them to say no, she'd held back, defensive, preparing herself for the rejection she feared was coming. And so it always came.

In San Francisco she was opening up, approaching the bookshop owners with curiosity, always ready for the possibility they might say yes. And now they did. Maya was beginning to realise just how much power she had to create the circumstances of her life, good and bad.

That afternoon Maya sat on a bench in the Japanese Tea Garden, surrounded by cherry-blossom trees waiting to bloom, running streams and still lakes, golden carp making lazy figures of eight and lingering in patches of sunshine, statues of polished stone, little lawns of clipped grass, perfectly placed bonsai trees and great giant pagodas. The sky was a cloudless milky blue and a light confetti of autumn leaves sprinkled splashes of sunset across the garden.

Maya, sank into the tranquillity that surrounded her, resting on the smooth wood, completely peaceful, watching the visitors meander by. Couples strolled along the paths, hand in hand, but it no longer made Maya sad to see other people in love. She'd stopped needing chocolate to cheer her up, and money to make her feel safe and successful. And now Maya no longer needed a man, to know she was lovable.

Maya couldn't leave the garden. Every time she tried to get up her body wouldn't follow. All it wanted to do was sit and watch. Eventually Maya moved to a bench that overlooked a garden of bonsai trees encircling a pond and a small stone bridge, overgrown with sunset ivy. With the exception of the mountains in Arizona, it was one of the most beautiful things Maya had ever seen. And she thanked God that her life, with all its ups and downs, had brought her to this place.

Maya realised she was hungry. She hadn't noticed before because her heart was full, and her spirit and soul were completely contented. Maya thought perhaps she should get up to find food, but her heart wanted to stay. So she waited, still captivated by the beauty around her and the sense of peace that sat inside her.

A few moments later someone sat down on the bench beside her. Maya turned to see Ben from the bookshop.

'Oh, hello.' Maya smiled, surprised. 'Why… what are you doing here?'

Ben looked at her, about to bite into a sandwich.

'I mean, I wasn't expecting to see you,' Maya stumbled on. 'But it is your city, so of course you're entitled to be here.'

'Why, thank you.' Ben smiled. 'I often come here. I love the colours in the fall.'

'It's beautiful,' Maya said, trying not to look too deeply into his brown eyes.

'Yes,' he said, looking at her. 'It is.'

Secretly smiling, and scared she might inadvertently kiss him, Maya focused on her feet with such attention that all the secrets of the universe might have been inscribed on them.

'Hey, we've sold all your books.'

'What!' Maya squealed, instantly looking up. 'Are you serious?'

'Yep.'

'Did you buy them all?'

Ben laughed. 'Why would I do that?'

'Yes. No, of course not. I just can't believe it!'

'I did read it, though.'

'You did? But you probably didn't… I mean, I doubt it's your kind of book. It's really for women. I wrote it for myself…'

'I know,' Ben said, 'but I loved it.'

Maya grinned, unable to speak.

'And I liked learning about your life. It's quite an inspiration.'

'Really?' Maya looked at her feet again. 'Um, well, thank you.'

'Can you give me a bunch more?'

'Yes! Of course. Absolutely. Do you think you'll sell them?'

'Oh, I know I will. I've already got five people on a waiting list.'

Maya couldn't believe it. She wanted to leap onto the bench and jump up and down. She wanted to grab Ben's hand and start dancing. She wanted to kiss him. Instead she just grinned.

'Wow,' Maya said, 'that's wonderful.'

Another piece of the puzzle fell into place. It was just as everyone had told her: it had taken compassion first, then courage, and finally connection. And now, reaping the rewards of learning these lessons, Maya was starting to live the life of her dreams.

After the garden, Maya and Ben spent the evening walking along the harbour. In addition to being extremely attractive, Ben was also sweet, thoughtful and very funny. He asked a lot of questions, with genuine interest, waiting to see what she might say. She noticed that he listened, really listened, without offering opinions or witty comments, or clever little insights that would say more about him than her. When she spoke he watched her as though she was the only other person on Earth. And he shared himself, with an honesty and openness that surprised and delighted her.

Maya told Ben almost everything about herself, but held back from sharing her attraction to him. Her newfound centredness still felt soft and fragile, and she didn't dare jeopardise it by jumping into anything with Ben. She'd learnt that lesson with

Jake. Besides, Maya knew she'd be leaving in three days, so there wasn't much point in courting that kind of heartbreak.

But that night she couldn't stop thinking about him and the thoughts crept into her dreams.

The next day Maya brought Ben another twenty copies, walking into the bookshop just as he was designing a window display for them. He'd scattered gold chocolate coins around a bookstand, above which he'd placed a goofy picture of himself.

'So, you're representing the men, are you?' Maya laughed. 'That's cute.'

'"Cute"?' Ben smiled. 'You've been here three weeks, and you're already turning into an American.'

'I do love it here,' Maya admitted, handing him a pile of books from her rucksack.

'Well, that's good. Have you decided where you'll go next?'

'Up to Portland, I think. A friendly bloke on a bus told me they have loads of alternative bookshops up there, just like this one.'

'Hey, less of that. We're one in a million.'

'Oh.' Maya smiled. 'I know you are.'

Soon it was the end of the week and Maya was leaving the next day. That night Ben cooked her a goodbye dinner. Over a delicious butternut squash and bacon soup, Maya told Ben about her brief love affair with Arizona and how she promised herself she'd go back.

'Hey, if you don't mind hanging around here for a few more days I'll take you there,' Ben said. 'Then you can catch a bus up to Portland.'

'Really? Are you serious?'

'You ask that a lot.' Ben smiled. 'And yes, I am.'

'Well, wow. That'd be… fantastic. Thank you. Why are going there?'

'I need to visit a few investors. I'm hoping to open another store.'

'That's fantastic, then you could sell my books all over America,' Maya joked.

Ben looked at her happily, and Maya smiled to herself. A year ago she'd have thought saying something like that was ridiculous at best, and unbearably arrogant at worst. Now it just felt wonderful.

'This is absolutely the best soup I've ever tasted,' May said. 'Who'd have thought that good food could be better than chocolate?'

'Wait until you try my sea bass,' Ben replied, smiling. 'And my pesto pasta.'

Three days later Maya was driving across the Arizona desert in Ben's battered red truck. As she sped along the highway, going far too fast, her hair flicking out behind her, Maya thought back to ten years ago, when she'd first watched *Thelma and Louise*. Ever since that day she'd dreamt of this.

It was as if, having learnt her lessons, the universe was now pouring gifts into her lap, giving Maya things she hadn't even remembered asking for. Maya whooped with joy and Ben laughed.

'Hey, are you hungry?' he asked.

Maya nodded, though she didn't want to slow down for a second.

'There's a great little taco place a few miles down Route 66.'

'Sounds fantastic.'

With Ben she was seeing and tasting all kinds of things she'd never have known about without him. Maya thought how glorious it was to connect with so many people and get so much help. She could hardly believe she'd struggled through her whole life without it.

Within half an hour they were sitting in the red leather booth of a cheerfully cheap diner, eating fajitas and looking out onto the mountains.

'This is delicious.' Maya grinned, dropping guacamole on her T-shirt and licking it off with her finger.

'For such a slim little thing, you certainly enjoy your food,' Ben said.

'Well, I don't try to starve and then stuff myself any more,' Maya explained. 'I used to spend my life sitting on a chair in a café, eating instead of living. Now I just live, and eat whatever I like, whenever I like. I don't think about it now, or second-guess myself, or hate myself. It's wonderful.'

Ben smiled. 'Well, I'm glad you're not a dieter.'

'Yeah,' Maya said, laughing, 'me too.'

That night they stayed in a motel, in separate beds. Neither had spoken a word about their feelings for each other, and Maya vowed she wouldn't be the one to bring it up. But there was something else she'd been thinking about for a while and wanted to ask.

Ever since Thomas had told her about the veil of Maya, about living in illusion and not seeing the truth, she'd wanted to change her name, to have it reflect the transformation she'd undergone herself.

She no longer lived in illusion. She was no longer dominated by worries, fear and low self-esteem. And Maya wanted her name to reflect that.

'Will you call me May?' she asked, just as Ben was about to turn off the light.

'Sure.'

'My cousin often calls me May anyway, so it's not a big deal,' she went on. 'It's my favourite month, and it's spring. It could represent my rebirth.'

'You don't need to explain,' Ben smiled. 'I'd call you Fred if it mattered to you.'

As she fell asleep May thought, for about the millionth time that day, that Ben was one of the loveliest people she'd ever met, and wondered if there was any chance he felt the same about her.

$\mathcal{T}$he next day they drove off the highway, rattling onto a dirt track that cut through the mountains. May gazed out at the beautiful red rocks, wishing she could reach out and touch them. They followed the path, each absorbed in the scenery, until Ben spoke.

'I'm taking you to Zion National Park.'

'Wonderful,' May said, having never heard of it, but thinking the name alone promised magical things.

Ben turned the next corner, driving into a clearing and parking the car. May opened her door and jumped out, kicking up a puff of red powder that settled on her flip-flops. Ben headed towards the nearest mountain.

'Follow me.'

May hurried after him, kicking up dust.

'There's a cliff I want to take you to,' Ben said, reaching for her hand. 'You have to walk up it alone, and it's said that when you stand at the top you'll get a message from God.'

'Really? How fantastic.'

They walked along valleys, cutting through the red cliffs and wandering past waterfalls, until finally they reached Angel's Landing.

May turned to Ben, who was already looking at her.

'So, now I have to go up alone?'

Ben nodded. 'But I have to give you something, before you go.'

'I hope it's a safety harness.' May smiled, looking up at the cliff.

Then he kissed her.

Eventually they just looked at each other. Ben touched her cheek.

'I'm yours, you know,' he said.

The words hung between them, floating in the air, hovering between the mountains. And despite how far she'd come, despite all she'd learnt, and how she loved herself now, May still couldn't quite believe it.

'But, you… I… we… I haven't done anything special… I'm not…'

Ben only smiled at her.

'May,' he said softly, 'you are magnificent.'

May stood at the peak of Angel's Landing and looked out at the mountain tops reaching up into the sky, to the distance of the desert, until she could no longer see its edge. Joy filled her heart, and excitement flooded her body.

She felt the air vibrating, the pulse of life rushing through her fingertips, and laughter rising up inside her. She knew she needed nothing more. She had everything. She was everything. She was completely alone, and yet she'd never felt more connected in her whole life.

As she stood at the edge of the cliff May knew, she absolutely knew, that nothing would ever be the same again. She lifted her arms into the air and tipped her head to gaze up at the sky. She watched the clouds float past until she had a clear view of the heavens. May smiled, tears filling her eyes.

'Thank you,' she whispered. 'Thank you.'

Recipes and Real Life

Before finding the consistent amounts of courage needed to wholeheartedly follow my own dreams, food (especially chocolate) and its effects were a painful obsession of mine. My attempts to resist, and inevitably over-consume it, ate up a lot of my creative energy.

Of course I criticised and berated myself constantly for this, always wondering what on earth was wrong with me. But in the end, to my great surprise, I discovered it was quite simple: there was nothing wrong with me, I just wasn't living a life I loved.

When I addressed this, when I became brave enough to be true to my heart and stop believing my mind (still a challenge and a choice every day!), the 'food issue' took care of itself.

I still have to be aware of my habits. Whenever I'm gripped by fear or start succumbing to negative thoughts, I naturally gravitate towards the fridge. But when I'm writing, singing, dancing, laughing and living from my heart I don't give my stomach a single thought.

I wish the very same experience for you and do hope that this book has helped you to love your body and let yourself off the hook, and encouraged you to obsess about your happiness instead of your calories!

In that spirit, I'd like to share some of my very favourite foods (according to the seasons I usually like to eat them) with you...

The savoury recipes were invented by Artur de sa Barreto, my extremely talented husband, without whom I would most certainly be malnourished. And the sweet recipes were specially created by the chef Jack van Praag, who is also my brother and my personal supplier of all things decadent and delicious.

Spring

RECIPES

Chilli Pesto Pasta

I wasn't a fan of pesto until I had it home-made. Artur's recipe is the best I've ever tasted, so we get through rather a lot of basil plants in the spring and summer months. The chillies (home-grown by husband) aren't spicy enough to stand out, but do wonders for the other flavours.

SERVES 2

FOR THE PESTO
30G BASIL LEAVES
1 CLOVE OF GARLIC, CHOPPED
90ML OLIVE OIL
30G PINE NUTS
1 SMALL MILD RED CHILLI
½ TEASPOON SALT
¼ TEASPOON BLACK PEPPER
½ TEASPOON GRANULATED SUGAR
35G PARMESAN, CUT INTO CUBES
1 TEASPOON BALSAMIC VINEGAR (21-YEAR-OLD IF POSSIBLE)

3 NESTS OF ANGEL HAIR PASTA OR VERMICELLI

- To combine the pesto ingredients use a food mixer if you have one, but a coffee grinder works just as well! Add the basil, balsamic vinegar, garlic, olive oil, pine nuts and chilli, and mix together. Add salt, pepper and sugar. Add the parmesan and mix again.

- Cook the pasta for 3 minutes until al dente. Drain and serve. Allow to cool for a moment before topping with the pesto sauce.

Lavender-Sugar Doughnuts

Fresh doughnuts have to be one of the most delicious treats around. Their warmth in your hands, the sweet smell of sugar, and the fried dough: crispy on the outside, soft in the middle... They aren't the easiest things in the world to make, but, since bought ones never come close to the perfection you can create at home, I think they're certainly worth the effort!

MAKES 16

SINGLE SPRIG OF FRESH
LAVENDER
200G CASTER SUGAR

170ML MILK
12G FRESH YEAST
90G CASTER SUGAR
500G PLAIN BREAD FLOUR
PINCH OF SALT
½ VANILLA POD
30G BUTTER, DICED
2 EGGS
VEGETABLE OIL, FOR FRYING

The lavender sugar

*   Cut up the sprig of fresh lavender. Add to 200g of sugar in an airtight container and leave for several days before use.

*   *Tip*: Lavender doesn't actually come into season until June, so if you're making the doughnuts at other times of the year, you can always use vanilla sugar or cinnamon instead.

The doughnuts

*   All the ingredients should be at room temperature. Pour the milk into a small bowl, add the yeast, 90g of caster sugar, 125g of flour and stir. Leave to stand. Sieve the rest of the flour into a large bowl, then add the salt, scraped-out seeds from the vanilla pod and butter and eggs. Add the milk mixture and combine.

- Turn the dough out onto a surface and knead until smooth and elastic. You might need to add a little extra flour at this point. Depending on your efforts, this should take about 10 minutes. Shape the dough into a ball and cover with a damp cloth until it doubles in size. Doughnut dough is even tastier if it's left in the fridge overnight, but it depends on how impatient you're feeling...

- Knead the dough again until it's back to its original size. Roll out on a floured surface to a thickness of 3mm. At this point cut out your doughnut shapes. It's best to cut the doughnuts into squares, rather than circles, because it'll make cooking them a lot easier. Leave to prove again until the dough doubles in size.

- Heat a deep saucepan with an inch of oil to 170°C. (You'll need to adjust and check the heat regularly with a cooking thermometer.) Fry the doughnuts until very lightly golden, then roll them in the lavender sugar and leave to cool for a few minutes. Eat immediately!

- *Safety note*: Be very careful, hot oil is dangerous. It can spit, burn and catch fire.

Summer

RECIPES

Sea Bass in White Wine and Butter Sauce

Artur and I eat this every Sunday afternoon during the summer. The flavours are so subtle and simple, and the fish so delicate, that it really does melt in the mouth. And it's all incredibly healthy, which is a wonderful bonus.

SERVES 2

2 FRESH SEA BASS FILLETS
50ML EXTRA VIRGIN OLIVE OIL
75ML DRY WHITE WINE
1 TABLESPOON WHITE WINE VINEGAR
1 TEASPOON SEA SALT
1 HEAD OF GARLIC
1 SMALL MILD RED CHILLI
6 MEDIUM POTATOES
OREGANO
85G BUTTER
100ML MILK
SALT AND BLACK PEPPER
150G CURLY KALE

• Wash the sea bass fillets and dry them. Place them in a shallow pan and marinate them in the olive oil, white wine, vinegar and salt. Finely chop the garlic and chilli and add to the marinade. Turn the fillets to make sure they're evenly coated. If you have the time, marinate them for 1 hour, but for no less than 20 minutes. (If you marinate the fillets for longer than 20 minutes, cover them and put in the fridge.)

• Boil the potatoes, with a sprinkling of oregano and salt in the water, until soft. Drain the potatoes. Melt 40g of butter in another pan and add the milk. Bring to simmer, then add the potatoes to the hot milk. Heat for 3 to 4 minutes and season with a little salt and pepper. Take off the heat and mash the potatoes until creamy.

- For the sauce, melt 25g of butter in a small saucepan. Add the marinade sauce to the pan and leave it to simmer for about 10 minutes.

- While the potatoes are cooking, bring a pan of water to boil to cook the curly kale, which will take approximately 2 to 3 minutes.

- Heat a non-stick frying pan on a medium heat. Melt 20g of butter and fry the fillets, skin-side down, for 3 minutes. Turn and cook for another 2 minutes. They may need a little longer, depending on the size of the fillets. You can tell the sea bass is ready when the flesh is white all the way through.

- Turn the fish onto a plate, with the potatoes and kale. Tip the sauce from the small saucepan into the frying pan (used to cook the fish) and simmer for 1 minute. Pour the sauce over the fish and serve.

- *Tip*: In the absence of sea bass, tilapia also goes beautifully with this sauce.

Maple Cinder Toffee Ice Cream

Ice cream is the perfect accompaniment to a summer afternoon, morning or evening. While chef van Praag makes the most incredible array of flavours, I particularly love this one because of its contrasting textures. The combination of the cool, creamy ice cream with the crispy cinder toffee and hot melted chocolate is nothing less than a taste sensation.

THE CINDER TOFFEE
20G LIQUID GLUCOSE
(AVAILABLE IN MOST
CHEMISTS AND SOME
SUPERMARKETS)
80G MAPLE SYRUP
175G CASTER SUGAR
130ML WATER
6G BICARBONATE OF SODA

THE ICE CREAM
400ML FULL-FAT MILK
600ML DOUBLE CREAM
5 EGG YOLKS
115G CASTER SUGAR
1½ VANILLA PODS

The cinder toffee

- Pour the glucose into a deep saucepan (otherwise the mixture might escape onto your oven top when you add the bicarbonate of soda), using a hot spoon to extricate the sticky stuff if necessary. Add the maple syrup, sugar and water and stir together. Bring to the boil (without stirring again) on a medium heat. With a sugar thermometer, check the temperature and remove from heat at 146°C. (If it goes above 150°C it'll burn and taste horrible.)

- Immediately add the bicarbonate of soda and whisk vigorously, but very carefully to avoid explosions as it'll rise quickly. Tip the mixture into a non-stick container (18cm x 18cm), preferably made of silicone. Alternatively you can use an oiled baking tin. Leave to cool at room temperature for an hour or so.

- *Tip*: In the event of any cinder toffee explosions on your work surfaces or utensils, it can be easily removed with boiling water.

- *Tip*: This cinder toffee will melt on your tongue. If you like it a little chewier, add just another 5g of liquid glucose.

The ice cream

- Mix the milk and cream together in a pan, bring to steam (the stage just before simmering) and add the seeds scraped from the vanilla pods. Take off the heat. Beat together the eggs and sugar in a bowl until light. Pour in the hot milk, while continuing to beat. Return the mixture to a gentle heat in a clean pan. Stir until it reaches a thickness to coat the back of a wooden spoon.* Ensure there are no lumps but be careful not to scramble the eggs. Sieve the mixture into a cold bowl.

- Pour into an ice-cream machine and churn until almost set. Then add the cinder toffee, chopped into small pieces, and leave until set. Serve with melted chocolate.

- *Tip*: If you don't have an ice-cream machine you can still do very well without! Simply pour the ice cream into a plastic container (with a lid) and pop into the freezer. Remove after 30 minutes and whisk until smooth. Return to freezer and repeat this procedure 3 to 4 times every 30 minutes until the ice cream is completely frozen and smooth. Add the cinder toffee at the late stages, after the last whisk through but before it's completely set.

- * When you're stirring the mixture over a gentle heat, to ensure the eggs have been pasteurised (and thus avoiding potential salmonella) they need to be heated to 72°C for 5 minutes.

Autumn

RECIPES

Butternut Squash and Bacon Soup

My husband, Artur, has an extensive, and always spontaneous, repertoire of soups, the recipes for which I collect in a notebook that lives in our kitchen cupboard. This is one I demand he makes every day of December. Being Portuguese, he usually tops the otherwise vegetarian flavours with bacon, but the soup is just as delicious with almonds instead.

SERVES 4

KNOB OF SALTED BUTTER
3 TABLESPOONS OLIVE OIL
1 MEDIUM BUTTERNUT
SQUASH, DICED
1 HEAD OF GARLIC, CHOPPED
TURMERIC
MILD CHILLI POWDER
PAPRIKA
1 PARSNIP, DICED
2 CUBES VEGETABLE STOCK
1½ LITRES WATER
2 MEDIUM POTATOES, DICED
100ML MILK
50G PARMESAN
SALT AND BLACK PEPPER,
FOR SEASONING
OPTIONAL: 3 RASHERS OF
BACON OR A HANDFUL OF
SLICED ALMONDS

- Add the olive oil and knob of butter to a deep saucepan. Melt the butter, then add the butternut squash and garlic. Next, add turmeric and mild chilli powder and paprika to taste. On medium heat, stir until soft and golden.

- Add the parsnip and stir. Dissolve the stock cubes in 1½ litres of boiling water, and add one third to the pan. Add the potatoes. Bring to boil and add the rest of the stock. Leave to simmer on medium heat until all the vegetables are soft. Turn down the heat and add the milk. Cook for 5 minutes.

- Blend the soup in the pan with a hand blender. Add parmesan, salt and pepper to taste. Leave the flavours to infuse for 10 minutes before serving.

- To serve, top the soup with crispy bacon (finely chopped) or sprinkle with sliced almonds.

Wild Honey and Damson Truffles

I adore chocolate truffles and these are absolutely gorgeous. Amazingly, they're also really easy to make (though perfecting the recipe in the first place wasn't – I had the very arduous task of eating A LOT of test truffles!) and of course are very much worth it.

MAKES ABOUT 50 TRUFFLES

210ML WATER
3 TABLESPOONS MILD WILD HONEY
240G UNSALTED BUTTER
400G CHOCOLATE (AT LEAST 72% COCOA)
40 DAMSONS (OR SOUR CHERRIES), STONED AND SLICED
A LITTLE COCOA POWDER TO COAT

- Heat the water and honey together, simmer lightly then remove from heat. Add the butter and stir in the chocolate. Stir thoroughly before adding the damsons. Pour into a baking tin (about 18cm x 25cm) and chill for two hours or until set.

- Remove from fridge and cut into squares. Roll them in cocoa powder before eating…

Winter

RECIPES

Portuguese-Style Chicken Soup

Wherever I am when I eat this soup it always takes me straight back to my mother-in-law's kitchen in Madeira – a very lovely place to be. If you can find the authentic spices, then you'll be transported to Portugal too. But it's still very lovely without.

SERVES 4 PEOPLE, OR 2 HUNGRY PEOPLE

55ML VEGETABLE OIL
4 PIECES OF CHICKEN (LEGS OR BREASTS)
1 TABLESPOON RED PAPRIKA (BETTER YET, **COLORAU**)
1 TEASPOON MILD CHILLI POWDER (BETTER YET, **PIMENTA MOIDA**)
2 BAY LEAVES
1 HEAD OF GARLIC, CHOPPED
1 MEDIUM TOMATO, CHOPPED
1 TABLESPOON TOMATO PUREE
1 MEDIUM WHITE ONION, SLICED
SALT, TO SEASON
50ML DRY WHITE WINE
1½ LITRES WATER
5 MEDIUM POTATOES, CHOPPED
4 CARROTS, CHOPPED
200G PEAS

Heat the vegetable oil in a deep saucepan, then add the chicken along with the spices, bay leaves, garlic, tomato and tomato puree, onions and salt. Stir vigorously so the chicken is evenly coated. Fry for about 8 minutes, until the onions are soft. Add the wine and cook for another 5 minutes before adding the water and then bring to the boil. Add the potatoes. When potatoes are nearly cooked, add the carrots. Allow to simmer for another 7 minutes. Finally add the peas. Cook for another 2 to 3 minutes. Turn off heat and let it cool for a few minutes before serving.

Chocolate Flapjacks

If I had to choose only one chocolate-related recipe to last me the rest of my life, this would be it. I can never stop after one, and I defy you to do so. For a truly heavenly experience, eat on a winter's night with a cup of hot chocolate, snuggled on the sofa in front of the fire.

MAKES 16, BUT HOW MANY IT SERVES DEPENDS ON HOW GENEROUS YOU'RE FEELING...

220G UNSALTED BUTTER
1 VANILLA POD
280G SOFT BROWN SUGAR
4 TABLESPOONS GOLDEN SYRUP
PINCH OF SALT
60G GOOD-QUALITY COCOA POWDER
300G LARGE ROLLED OATS

- Melt the butter in a saucepan, then take off the heat and scrape the vanilla seeds into the pan. Drop the pod in too and leave to infuse for half an hour. Remove the vanilla pod and put the pan back onto a low heat, then add the sugar, syrup, salt and cocoa. Simmer and stir for 5 minutes. Add the oats and mix together. (Try not to eat too much of the raw mixture!)

- Pour the flapjack mixture into a baking tin and pat it down to a thickness of ¾ inch. Bake for 25 minutes at 150°C. Remove from the oven, cut into squares and cool on wire rack before eating.

With love and thanks to ...

My husband, Artur, whose generosity, humour, sweetness and brilliance make me grateful every day. My mum, Vicky, a neverending source of faith, wisdom, joy and inspiration. My dad, David, for his love, his literary genes and for once saying I was born to be a writer. My brother, Jack, who fills my heart with happiness and my belly with his gourmet genius. My grandparents, Arnold and Fay, for loving, listening and being such wonderful role models in always staying true to their dreams. Christine, who took us under her wing and into her heart, the most loving step-mum a girl could hope to have. Ray, a step-dad who sacrificed so much, thank you for your kind heart. My sweet Idilia, who became an instant soulmate and constant cheerleader. My gorgeous cousin Lucy for her loving heart and open mind. My aunt Kathy for her encouragement and support since the beginning. Steph, Celso, Mark and Alan for bringing me into their family. Mai and Pai for accepting and loving me unconditionally.

My very first editors: Timma, Nanette, Katia, Angela and P.K. And all my initial readers: Idilia, Valerie, Hazel, Rosie N., Hilli, Heike, Kelly-Jo, Jodi, Holly, Fern, Abi, Susan, Josh W., Alisa, Julie, Yolanda, Karen H., Ursula, Katja, Colleen, Jaime, Cindee, Isabelle, Dorothy, Alex, Britta, Antje, Rosie A., Sandra, Vicky and Mark. Your contributions were invaluable.

Extra special thanks to Ariel and Shya Kane for all their incredible wisdom, insight, inspiration and compassion. You are two miracles in my life, and gifts to the world. Without you both there would be no book – thank you, thank you, thank you! And to the rest of the Transformational community (not mentioned above) who are all so inspiring: Stephan & Maiken, Stefanie & Rainer, Rod & Caitlin, Amy & Andy, Marie & Josh, Mac & Ellen, Ralf & Arne, Joe & Lenore, Harry & Annette, Britt & Frank, Tricia & Sue, Bill & Charlotte, Claudia & Bernd, Dorina & Norman, John, Karen L., Tony, Stefanie E., Stefanie H., Andy S., Sandy, Andrea, Elfi, Terri,

Livia, Elke, Tanja, Christina, Sonja, Carola, Heidi, Henning, Katrin, Sue D., Susan F., Colleen, Ulf, Jessica, Stan – and all the other wonderful folks I've foolishly forgotten...

My dear friend Stefanie, who gave her great talent and precious time to designing the first cover of the book and the beautiful website. And the incredible Fernanda Franco, who designed the original artwork on which the current cover is based. You made me very happy indeed.

Fellow writers Penny, Katia and Laurence for being so wonderfully talented, endlessly supportive and always honest – you are the best writing group and the loveliest friends I could hope for. Dave for his generosity of spirit, for always being there, and for setting the bar so high!

And to more friends far and wide: gorgeous Val, for so much fun!; Rachelle for taking such care of me; Ben for his unconditional love; Har Hari for nourishing my soul; Steve B. for his time, wisdom and support; Simon S. for being a haven at Oxford; Prince Thomas for always saying yes; Jules for being the best buddy ever; Jack for being such a bright light and big heart; Nashy for all the fun and free cinema trips; Paul for being incredibly loyal and lovely; Lotte for being my first, most wonderful dance teacher; Rosie for all the lazy café afternoons and writing fun; Jaime for her compassion; Hazel for all the hot chocolate; Rosie Pie for the entire cake and Marilyn days; Melissa for being such a longtime friend; Krishna for his insight and inspiration; Emma for her laughter; Alice and Cosi for their kickboxing skills; Morgan for her cookie and cream cupcakes; Martin T. for all his many kindnesses; Al for knocking me out; Alex C. for making office life almost bearable; M.J. for her enthusiasm; Juliette for her yoga giggles; Oksana for being so sweet and generous; Pam, David W., Louise C., Alice R., Miriam, Francois S., Paul S., Don A., the Cambridge Lindy Hoppers; Matt and Lotte, Katherine, Gill, Bill, Maria, Gerald, Mirjana, Sam, Natalie, Lara, Barney, Toni, Gemma, Will, Liz and James, Robert, Ros, Colin, Mike, Asif, Claire, Holly and Alex.

Big thanks to Katie Fford and Fiona Walker for their kindness and generosity in reading the work of an unknown writer. And Sophie and Audrey Boss for doing the same. Kate Osborne for supporting the self-published version and providing encouragement during the hard times. Alice Ryan, for being so sweet, kind and talented. Louise, a lovely and generous soul.

Hannah, Simon, Andy and Helen at Borders, Cambridge, for loving the book and believing in it from the beginning. Klaus at Watkins, Brian at David's and all at Ark for their generosity in taking a chance on a newbie.

All my magnificent teachers: Jeff and Julie for first opening my heart, Carol Stewart for being so inspiring she even made me love Chaucer, and Simon Skinner, Maurice Keen, Martin Conway and John Davis for all their patience, shared wisdoms and ineffable amounts of kindness and generosity.

Last, and absolutely not least, to the entire Hay House team for bringing this book into the world and spreading its message more widely than I ever could alone. Eternal gratitude to Michelle for believing in the book, to Alexandra for doing the most amazing job selling it to the rest of the world, to Wendy and Joanna for perfecting the manuscript, to Leanne for her beautiful designs, to Jo and Louise for all their wonderful publicity efforts, and to Amanda for her amazing amounts of enthusiasm, constant support and superhuman patience over my endless emails! I couldn't have found a better home for the book. Thank you.

Notes

Notes

Notes

Notes

We hope you enjoyed this Hay House book.
If you would like to receive a free catalogue featuring additional
Hay House books and products, or if you would like information
about the Hay Foundation, please contact:

Hay House UK Ltd
292B Kensal Rd • London W10 5BE
Tel: (44) 20 8962 1230; Fax: (44) 20 8962 1239
www.hayhouse.co.uk

***

Published and distributed in the United States of America by:
Hay House, Inc. • PO Box 5100 • Carlsbad, CA 92018-5100
Tel.: (1) 760 431 7695 or (1) 800 654 5126;
Fax: (1) 760 431 6948 or (1) 800 650 5115
www.hayhouse.com

Published and distributed in Australia by:
Hay House Australia Ltd • 18/36 Ralph St • Alexandria NSW 2015
Tel.: (61) 2 9669 4299; Fax: (61) 2 9669 4144
www.hayhouse.com.au

Published and distributed in the Republic of South Africa by:
Hay House SA (Pty) Ltd • PO Box 990 • Witkoppen 2068
Tel./Fax: (27) 11 467 8904 • www.hayhouse.co.za

Published and distributed in India by:
Hay House Publishers India • Muskaan Complex • Plot No.3
B-2 • Vasant Kunj • New Delhi – 110 070.
Tel.: (91) 11 41761620; Fax: (91) 11 41761630.
www.hayhouse.co.in

Distributed in Canada by:
Raincoast • 9050 Shaughnessy St • Vancouver, BC V6P 6E5
Tel.: (1) 604 323 7100; Fax: (1) 604 323 2600

***

Sign up via the Hay House UK website to receive the Hay House
online newsletter and stay informed about what's going on with
your favourite authors. You'll receive bimonthly announcements
about discounts and offers, special events, product highlights,
free excerpts, giveaways, and more!
www.hayhouse.co.uk